This study takes a look at end time events and is a verse-by-verse commentary on the book of Revelation. No one can set an exact date on when the end will come but because of God's track record on fulfilling prophecy we know the end is coming. But we also know for sure the end will really be the beginning of great things! While end time events we know will happen the exact placement on God's timeline is not always clear. We often get bogged down in the symbolism and miss the wonderful message of this fascinating book. So to study Revelation with understanding place the events you are not sure of the time around the events that have fixed times. As you study look for the blessings — Jesus is coming after His Church; God is giving Christ authority to judge sin and the injustices of life; the Church will glory in her relationship with Christ; and all in Heaven will worship God throughout eternity. Hallelujah! Satan and sin will be defeated and punished throughout eternity — Glory to God! What a blessing.

UNDERSTANDING THE BOOK OF REVELATION

A simple study of end times and verse by verse study of Revelation

David Baxley, D. Min.

Equip Press
Colorado Springs, Colorado

UNDERSTANDING
THE BOOK OF
REVELATION

A simple study of end times and verse
by verse study of Revelation

Understanding the Book of Revelation:
A simple study of end times and verse by verse study of Revelation
Copyright © 2018 David Baxley, D. Min.
All rights reserved. No part of this publication may be reproduced, distributed, or transmitted in any form or by any means, without prior written permission.

Scripture quotations marked (ESV) are taken from *The ESV® Bible (The Holy Bible, English Standard Version®)* copyright © 2001 by Crossway, a publishing minis-try of Good News Publishers. ESV® Text Edition: 2011. The ESV® text has been reproduced in cooperation with and by permission of Good News Publishers. Unauthorized reproduction of this publication is prohibited. Used by permission. All rights reserved.

Scripture quotations marked (KJV) are taken from the *King James Bible*. Accessed on Bible Gateway at www.BibleGateway.com.

Scripture quotations marked (NASB) are taken from the *New American Standard Bible®* (NASB), copyright © 1960, 1962, 1963, 1968, 1971, 1972, 1973, 1975, 1977, 1995 by The Lockman Foundation, www.Lockman.org. Used by permission.

Scripture quotations marked (NIV) are taken from the *Holy Bible, New International Version*. Copyright © 1973, 1978, 1984, 2011 by Biblica, Inc.® Used by permission. All rights reserved worldwide.

Scripture quotations marked (NKJV) are taken from the *New King James Version®*. Copyright © 1982 by Thomas Nelson, Inc. Used by permission. All rights reserved.

Scripture quotations marked (NLT) are taken from the *Holy Bible, New Living Translation*, copyright © 1996, 2004, 2015 by Tyndale House Foundation. Used by permission of Tyndale House Publishers, Inc., Carol Stream, Illinois 60188. All rights reserved.

Scripture quotations marked (NRSV) are taken from the *New Revised Standard Version Bible*, copyright © 1989 the Division of Christian Education of the National Council of the Churches of Christ in the United States of America. Used by permission. All rights reserved.

First Edition: 2018
Understanding the Book of Revelation: A simple study of end times and verse by verse study of Revelation / David Baxley, D. Min.
Paperback ISBN: 978-1-946453-15-0
eBook ISBN: 978-1-946453-16-7

I dedicate this study to my Lord and Savior Jesus Christ for His Glory. And to my wife **AARONIA BAXLEY** for her steadfast love and help to me in life, in ministry and especially those days in the hospital when God blessed me with a new heart through a transplant.

PERSONAL NOTE: Consider becoming an organ donor. One donor can make up to 11 transplants possible. As a man whose physical life has been radically changed through the giving of another, I can tell you it makes a life changing difference. My heart was made available from the loss of another person's life and I sorrow for that family, yet because of their choice to donate organs, mine and several other lives were changed. In the midst of sorrows came a lasting living memorial to this individual. I thank God for His grace and strength during this process, and this second chance at life!

For more information on becoming a donor go to https://www.organdonor.gov.

David Baxley

TABLE OF CONTENTS

Introduction to End Time Events		9
Introduction to the Book of Revelation		37
Chapter 1	Revelation Chapter 1	39
Chapter 2	Revelation Chapters 2 & 3	43
Chapter 3	Revelation Chapter 4	55
Chapter 4	Revelation Chapter 5	59
Chapter 5	Revelation Chapter 6	63
Chapter 6	Revelation Chapter 7	67
Chapter 7	Revelation Chapter 8	73
Chapter 8	Revelation Chapter 9	77
Chapter 9	Revelation Chapter 10	85
Chapter 10	Revelation Chapter 11	87
Chapter 11	Revelation Chapter 12	93
Chapter 12	Revelation Chapter 13	99
Chapter 13	Revelation Chapter 14	105
Chapter 14	Revelation Chapter 15	111
Chapter 15	Revelation Chapter 16	113
Chapter 16	Revelation Chapter 17	119
Chapter 17	Revelation Chapter 18	123
Chapter 18	Revelation Chapter 19	127
Chapter 19	Revelation Chapter 20	133
Chapter 20	Revelation Chapter 21	139
Chapter 21	Revelation Chapter 22	145
Chapter 22	Summary of Revelation	149

UNDERSTANDING END TIME EVENTS AND THE BOOK OF REVELATION

The Events of the End Time

The book of Revelation gets mixed reactions from people. There's a certain sense of curiosity about the future, yet the book can be intimidating because of the futuristic symbolism used. In this amazing book, God offers a special blessing for all who read it, believe it, and practice what it says.

What are the blessings of Revelation? At the heart of the blessing is the assurance that Jesus is coming again and will bring judgement on evil and injustice. Then Jesus Christ will rule on earth with all believers during His millennial kingdom. This is a promise given to the Jews. After the millennial kingdom is over all believers will spend eternity with God! What a hope! God has a plan and is working it. Evil and injustice will be judged and believers will live with God forever!

The symbolism is used to demonstrate how severe divine judgment is going to be. When the symbolism and the sensational pictures of judgment becomes the focus of your study you miss the main message. To understand the book of Revelation it helps to have an understanding of the events of the end times. So consider these brief explanations about end time events.

Why are the woes of the tribulation so harsh? It will take these woes to cause Israel to finally recognize Jesus Christ as the promised Messiah. The woes are judgments of God because of the sin of the earth. God will use the woes as a means to vindicate saints who died because of their faith in Jesus and as a process of reclaiming possession of the earth from Satan.

God made some unconditional everlasting covenants with the nation of Israel. A covenant is an agreement between two parties. God always does what He says He will do, so we know all the covenants that God made will be completely fulfilled. Some of these covenants won't be totally fulfilled until the end times. Here are some of those covenants that were unconditional, meaning that God promised without consideration to performance:

THE ABRAHAMIC COVENANT (Gen. 12,15) God said that He would make Israel a blessing to the entire world. This was partially fulfilled with the birth of Jesus who was a descendant of Abraham (through Mary's lineage). It will be completely fulfilled as Jesus comes again to rule over the earth during the millennial kingdom.

THE LAND COVENANT (Gen. 13,15) This promises the nation of Israel possession of certain land. This covenant was partially fulfilled when Israel settled the land as Joshua led them out of the wilderness. They divided the land by tribes but they did not possess all of the Promised Land. It was not until the time of King David through his military conquests that they possessed the land that God had promised them. Soon after Solomon's reign was over the nation split to form Israel in the North and Judah in the South. Because of their disobedience to God, Israel was overtaken by the Assyrians and Judah by the Babylonians. They were scattered around the world until Israel came back to possess a portion of their land in 1948. Today they only possess a very small segment of what God has promised them but Israel will possess all her promised land in the millennial kingdom.

THE DAVIDIC COVENANT (2 Sam. 7) This covenant promises that the Messiah will rule from the throne of David. This covenant will be fulfilled during the millennial kingdom. God also promised that Israel would always be His covenant people, and they have been.

God gave certain conditional religious laws to Israel. These laws are conditional upon the Jews obedience in relation to God's blessings. These laws, dietary, civil and temple laws, are not given to the church age as such. The Law (the Ten Commandments) stands as God's standard of righteousness for all ages. It reveals that all are unrighteous and need forgiveness.

God's promise, His covenant to Israel is different from Christ's promise to the church. Everyone, Jews and Gentiles alike, are saved by the same process — faith in Jesus Christ alone. Up until the time of Christ, it was faith in the fact that the Messiah would come. After Christ's first coming it is faith in the fact that He did come and offered a complete sacrifice for our sins that saves us.

The Bible tells us that God suspended part of His work with Israel but it does not tell us that God's covenant with Israel has ceased. It is still in effect for them as an act of obedience. Just before or at the beginning of the first 3 1/2 years of the tribulation the temple will be rebuilt according to God's exact specification and sacrifices and festivals will resume. After the church is raptured God will lift His suspension and continue to primarily work with Israel much like in the Old Testament.

Remember, Jesus Christ is the basis for salvation and the sacrifices and festivals will be an act of obedience for the Jews, somewhat like water baptism is for Christians.

Jesus Christ's promises to New Testament Christians are different from God's promises to Israel. Christ promised the church that they would individually be given the Holy Spirit as He promised that the comforter would come (John 14:16–31). Jesus promised to come back and receive the church in the air where He will be when He calls. Then He will carry Christians on to heaven (John 14:2). Jesus also promised that in the meantime He would prepare a special place for His bride the church (Matthew 14:2). In Revelation 21:9 John is shown the new city of Jerusalem, which is identified as belonging to Christ's bride. Jesus said that New Testament believers (His bride) will rule and reign with Him during the millennial kingdom (Rev. 20:6). Jesus promised the church rewards for service motivated by obedience (Matt. 5:21; Luke 6:23).

Again, let me emphasize that salvation always has been by faith in Jesus Christ alone. The process of God's promises before eternity is different for the Old Testament saints than it is for New Testament saints. Yet all true believers will have the same eternal destination.

The unfulfilled promises to the Jews will be fulfilled through the tribulation into the millennial kingdom and then through eternity. The promises to the church will be fulfilled through the rapture into the millennial kingdom and then through eternity. Many Gentiles will be saved during the tribulation but God is primarily working with the Jews.

1. EVENTS OF THE END TIMES

A. **END TIME WARS.** Several wars will be fought during the end times.

THE PSALM 83 WAR. The war described in Psalm 83 is probably the first of these wars. It will be a war started by the neighboring countries who attack Israel to exterminate her. The prophets Zechariah (Zech. 12:6) and Amos (Amos 9:15) tell us that Israel will not be uprooted but will have a great victory. This victory gives Israel a great expansion in land and valuable resources. The Psalm 83 war sets up the next war which is described in Ezekiel 38 and 39. Ezekiel 39 says that it will take seven years to burn the weapons after this war so that war must be fought before the last seven years of the tribulation. The tribulation will be the last seven years of earth as we know it. So, the Psalm 83 war will be fought probably before the rapture and sometime before the Ezekiel war starts.

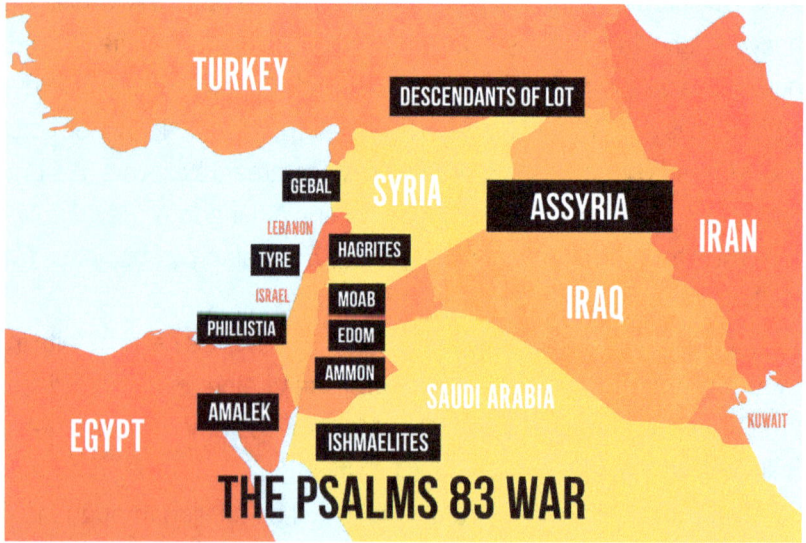

THE FIRST WAR OF GOG AND MAGOG. This war is described in Ezekiel 38 and 39. In a desire to capture the great oil fields that Israel has just won from the Psalm 83 war (Ezekiel 38:12 describe the wealth as the spoils of Israel), Russia makes a coalition with many other nations to invade Israel. Ezekiel 38:18–23 says that God will cause a great earthquake, pestilence, hail storm, fire, brimstone, and battlefield confusion which will give Israel the victory in this war. The world will see this victory as coming from the Lord! Ezekiel 39:9 says that it will take seven years to burn the weapons of war which means it will have to be fought before the seven years of the tribulation begins. Perhaps it is nuclear waste that will have to be buried, we don't know for sure. So this war is fought sometime before the beginning of the tribulation. Daniel 9:24–27 talks about the tribulation beginning with the Antichrist signing a covenant. This covenant is believed to be a peace treaty and signing such a covenant fits well at the end of the first war of Gog and Magog. This signing will officially begin seven years of tribulation. Below is a map of nation who will form a military coalition against Israel during the war of Gog and Magog.

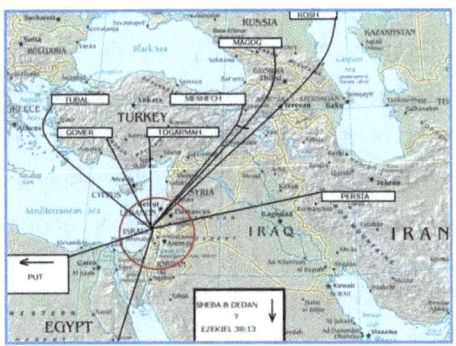

WAR OF REVELATION 8 AND 9. A war that could be a description of the nuclear battle of Gog and Magog or more likely another war fought just after the middle of the tribulation. When the Antichrist moves into Jerusalem he will break his own peace treaty with Israel and this war could be in retribution to the breaking of the treaty.

Revelation 9:15 says that the results of this war cause 1/3 of the world's population (approximately 1.5 billion) to be destroyed. Then in Revelation 16 it describes loathsome and malignant sores that will come upon people which seem to describe the effects of a nuclear war. More than likely this war will be fought during the first part of the last half of the tribulation.

The woes during the second half, probably the results of the war of Revelation 8 and 9, will cause Jewish believers to flee to a place in the "wilderness" where they will be supernaturally protected by God (Rev.). Many believe this hiding place will be the ancient city of Petra, located inside a box canyon in modern Jordan. These Jews will be safe there as Daniel 11 describes the Antichrist's defeats of all of the Middle East countries except Jordan.

Then the Antichrist will hear that kings from the East and the North are moving towards him. The Euphrates River will dry up so the King from the East and his army can easily get to Israel. When the Antichrist hears these kings are moving their armies towards him, he moves his army toward Megiddo to face them.

THE BATTLE OF ARMAGEDDON. As the armies of the world arrive around Megiddo to fight against Israel the battle of Armageddon will be fought (Joel 3; Zech. 14; and Rev. 19). This battle will be fought at the end of the tribulation. All armies will move toward Israel. As all of the armies of the world gather just outside of Israel Christ and His new bride will come from heaven to earth. This is His second coming. Christ will speak the word of God and it will slay all of the armies and kings of the world. Sin is defeated. Earth is reconstructed by fire and the effects from the curse of sin are gone. The Antichrist and false prophet will be cast in the lake of fire and Satan is chained in the bottomless pit. This ushers in the millennial kingdom.

THE SECOND BATTLE OF GOG AND MAGOG. This is a battle where Satan is released from his chains and from the bottomless pit. He immediately raises an army to fight against Christ. This battle will be fought in approximately the same area that the war of Ezekiel 38, 39, the first War of Gog and Mag was fought. Christ very quickly defeats Satan and he is cast into the lake of fire for eternity.

B. **THE RAPTURE.** The term rapture is used to describe Jesus descending from heaven into the air above the earth to call all church age believers to meet Him in the air. While this term is not used in the Bible, it is a word that describes the calling away of believers from earth to meet Christ in the air. The Apostle Paul was clear in his assurance to believers in Thessalonica that there is nothing that would prevent them as believers from seeing the glory of Christ in the sky.

1 Thessalonians 4:13–17 (NKJV) ¹³ But I do not want you to be ignorant, brethren, concerning those who have fallen asleep, lest you sorrow as others who have no hope. ¹⁴ For if we believe that Jesus died and rose again, even so God will bring with Him those who sleep in Jesus. ¹⁵ For this we say to you by the word of the Lord, that we who are alive *and* remain until the coming of the Lord will by no means precede those who are asleep. ¹⁶ For the Lord Himself will descend from heaven with a shout, with the voice of an archangel, and with the trumpet of God. And the dead in Christ will rise first. ¹⁷ Then we who are alive *and* remain shall be caught up together with them in the clouds to meet the Lord in the air. And thus we shall always be with the Lord.

A trumpet will sound, the archangel will shout, and dead believers will come with Jesus in the air. Believers who are still alive at the time will ascend into the sky to be with Jesus and believers of the church age who had already passed on. Everyone will be given a heavenly body and will go with Jesus into heaven. All this happens literally in a half-second as 1 Corinthians 15 says.

1 Corinthians 15:50–52 (NKJV) [50] Now this I say, brethren, that flesh and blood cannot inherit the kingdom of God; nor does corruption inherit incorruption. [51] Behold, I tell you a mystery: We shall not all sleep, but we shall all be changed — [52] in a moment, in the twinkling of an eye, at the last trumpet. For the trumpet will sound, and the dead will be raised incorruptible, and we shall be changed.

What will true believers still living actually see when the rapture occurs? Nothing, except the presence of Jesus. It happens so quickly there won't be time to mentally channel what's going on.

When will the rapture happen? At the end of the church age. The church age is the period of time after God partially suspended His work with Israel and Christ began working with the church. It began shortly after Jesus ascended into heaven. On the day of Pentecost when the Holy Spirit filled individual believers, the church was empowered for the ministry of the church. The church, individual believers, are agents which God uses to be a witness of Christ on earth. The church age will continue until the rapture when the church is taken out of this world. After the rapture God will resume work primarily with the Jews again in a manner similar to the Old Testament.

At the close of the first war of Gog and Magog, devastation, death and great famine will plague the earth. These conditions will mark the first part of the tribulation. It is understandable how these conditions would lead to great shortages of food and life's basic needs. These shortages make the rationing system of the Antichrist easy to understand. The Antichrist will declare that a person must take his mark, 666, on their forehead or wrist in order to purchase anything (Rev. 13:16–18).

There are debates about the exact place on God's timeline that the rapture will occur. Many believe in what is called **pre-tribulation rapture**. This simply teaches that the rapture will occur before the period of judgment (the tribulation) on the earth begins. There are several reasons given by those who choose this placement of the rapture.

One reason people believe in a pre-tribulation rapture is that when the church is raptured the restraining work of the Holy Spirit will be gone.

2 Thessalonians 2:6, 7 (NKJV) [6] And now you know what is restraining, that he may be revealed in his own time. [7] For the mystery of lawlessness is already at work; only He who now restrains *will do so* until He is taken out of the way.

The Holy Spirit working through the New Testament church is the present restrainer of evil on earth. The Holy Spirit's work was different in the Old Testament and will be different during the tribulation because the restrainer will be gone. The Holy Spirit's work of bringing conviction to the lost has always been around. The Holy Spirit as convictor will be present in the tribulation just as He was during the Old and New Testament times. During the church age The Holy Spirit lives in the hearts of believers and this is how He restrains how far evil can go. The church's presence teaches God's principles and moral restraints. When believers leave the earth, restraints on evil will be gone.

2 Thessalonians 2:3 (NKJV) ³ Let no one deceive you by any means; for *that Day will not come* unless the falling away comes first, and the man of sin is revealed, the son of perdition,

The reasoning is this: The rapture will happen before the Antichrist, who has already moved into the public eye and won't be able to bring the fullness of evil until the restrainer is gone. The Apostle Paul tells us that the Antichrist will come on the political scene before the church leaves earth. At the beginning of the tribulation, evil against believers will intensify and in the last half the woes will greatly increase. The restrainer will need to be gone before evil grows to this intensity.

The Bible (in Daniel 9:27) tells us that when the Antichrist signs a peace agreement, the tribulation (a seven year period of God's judgment on earth) will begin. When it begins the Antichrist will begin to reveal his evil. The Antichrist signing such an agreement at the conclusion of the first war of Gog and Magog fits.

The rapture could occur before the seven years of the tribulation begin, allowing the Antichrist as he comes to power, the freedom to begin executing evil. The depths of evil will greatly escalate during the second half of this seven year period.

A second reason many believe in a pre-tribulation rapture is because of God's promise. Paul says that God did not appoint the church to wrath but to obtain, or to complete, salvation through Jesus Christ.

1 Thessalonians 5:9–11 (NKJV) ⁹ For God did not appoint us to wrath, but to obtain salvation through our Lord Jesus Christ, ¹⁰ who died for us, that whether we wake or sleep, we should live together with Him.

It appears that the wrath of the tribulation was not appointed for the church, but the church would be with Christ forever. Also in:

Revelation 3:10 (NKJV) ¹⁰ Because you have kept My command to persevere, I also will keep you from the hour of trial which shall come upon the whole world, to test those who dwell on the earth.

One of Jesus' promises to the church at Philadelphia was that as believers they would not face the hour of trial that shall come upon the whole world. In other words they would not go through the tribulation.

Still others believe that the rapture will happen at the middle of the Tribulation period rather than at the beginning. This theory is called **mid-tribulation rapture**. There are several reasons why they place the rapture at the beginning of the last 3 1/2 years of earth.

One reason is this: at the beginning of the second half of the tribulation, the sounding of the trumpet as seen under the seventh seal occurs. Some see this trumpet as the same one that will sound at the rapture. The Bible doesn't say this specifically and really there is no reason to believe that this is the same trumpet except that in both places it says that a trumpet will sound.

Another reason people give for this theory is that the depths of woes on earth won't begin until the last 3 1/2 years of earth. Reasoning is that it takes the first 3 1/2 years to accomplish 2 Timothy 2:3 which says that the church must endure hardship before the end will come. Through effects of the wars of Psalm 83, and maybe through the Ezekiel 38 and 39 wars, the church might experience this hardship.

Some believe in a **post-tribulation rapture**, which is where the church will go through the entire tribulation and be raptured at the end to return with Christ. This theory does not fit with many scriptures like **1 Thessalonians 5:9–11** which says that the church won't go through the worst of the woes.

The rapture seems to fit better before the tribulation, leaving the first 3 1/2 years for the temple to be built and sacrifice reinstated before it is stopped at the middle of the tribulation. Where Christ places the rapture is not the focus. The assurance that the New Testament church will be raptured is the focus and a source of blessing to the believer.

C. **BELIEVERS GIVEN NEW BODIES.** For every true believer who dies, their soul goes into the safety and protection of Jesus in heaven. When the church is raptured, Christ will bring with Him the souls of all the dead from the church age according to 1 Thessalonians 4:13–14.

1 Thessalonians 4:13–14 (NKJV) ¹³ But I do not want you to be ignorant, brethren, concerning those who have fallen asleep, lest you sorrow as others who have no hope. ¹⁴ For if we believe that Jesus died and rose again, even so God will bring with Him those who sleep in Jesus.

In this passage Paul is addressing a fear by young Christians in Thessalonica who were concerned that those in the church who had died would miss the glory of Christ's coming. They are assured that all of the church will see the glory of the rapture.

1 Corinthians 15 tells us that our physical body, which is sown in corruption, because it is affected with sin, will be changed into a body that has not been affected by sin. The church at the rapture will all receive this new body. Christ brings with Him those New Testament saints who had already died and they along with those who are still alive when the rapture occurs will all be given spiritual bodies. Verses 50–52 tell us a little bit more about that change.

1 Corinthians 15:50–52 (NKJV) ⁵⁰ Now this I say, brethren, that flesh and blood cannot inherit the kingdom of God; nor does corruption inherit incorruption. ⁵¹ Behold, I tell you a mystery: We shall not all sleep, but we shall all be changed — ⁵² in a moment, in the twinkling of an eye, at the last trumpet. For the trumpet will sound, and the dead will be raised incorruptible and we shall be changed.

When will the Old Testament and tribulation believers get their new bodies? Their souls go to heaven when they die and it appears that they are in the same state that the dead New Testament believers were in before the rapture. When will the Old Testament saints be resurrected?

In Daniel 12:1–2 it says that Daniel's people, the Jews, whose names are written in the book, those saved in the Old Testament, will be delivered and then the multitudes who sleep in the dust will be awakened some to shame and contempt. Daniel was told that this resurrection would happen he just couldn't see that there would be 1,000 years separating the two parts — the resurrection of saved Jews and the resurrection of all who are not saved.

Old Testament saints along with tribulation saints who were martyred, those saved during the tribulation but killed because of their faith, will be resurrected at the end of the millennial reign of Christ and the beginning of eternity. Their souls are safely with God just like the souls of those who profess Christ are safe in God's protection before the rapture. Those saved during the tribulation will inhabit the earth around the new city of Jerusalem, which will be the nation of Israel. At this time, all of the curse and influence of sin has been cleansed from the earth and Satan is locked up for 1,000 years. If these Old Testament and Tribulation saints don't have their resurrection body in heaven right now what do they look like? It appears they have a body of some kind because the Rich Man recognized Lazarus. When John saw the saints under the altar in Revelation they cried out, which requires a body, but they were not with the church who were in their resurrected bodies. At the rapture we will all be changed and even though we are not told specifically how our soul will be housed until we receive our resurrection body, it appears that we will have a temporary body. The Old Testament saints, those saved before Christ arose, will wait until the end of the millennial kingdom to receive their resurrection body while the New Testament saints will receive their resurrection body at the rapture and the Tribulation saints will receive theirs at the end of the millennial reign.

D. Judgment **SEAT OF CHRIST/ BEMA SEAT**. Romans 14:10–12, and Corinthians 5:10 tell us that New Testament believers will stand before the judgment seat of Christ to be rewarded for acts of obedience while on the earth. The term "judgment seat" comes from the Greek word Bema which is why some refer to it as the Bema Seat judgment. It is called judgment seat because in the Roman world when someone stood before a judge, the judge was on a platform seated on a big chair, so it was referred to as standing before the judgment seat. Because of the term "judgment" people often misunderstand the nature of what will be judged here. This judgment does not judge salvation nor sin. Only believers will be at this judgment and a person's sin in his life has already been settled at their salvation. It is a time of reward for how faithfully the believer served Christ. 1 Corinthians 9:4–10, and 2 Timothy 2:5 talk about receiving crowns for various acts of obedience. The exact nature of the reward is not specifically given because that is not the focus. The promise of rewards for service is the focus. Again, we are not told when this will happen. Some believe it will happen at the death of each saint. Yet it seems to fit the timeline better to place it just after the rapture.

E. **THE ANTICHRIST.** Nearly everyone has heard of the Antichrist. He is known by several names in the Bible — Antichrist, Man of Sin, Son of Perdition, The Beast, A Little Horn, and False Christ. What is he? He will be human — generally thought to be a man though since the masculine pronoun can be used generically, it could be a woman. But who is he? Satan doesn't know when Jesus is going to rapture the church nor when the tribulation will begin because Satan is not omniscient. So it would make sense that Satan has groomed a person in every age ready to step into the position of the Antichrist. Because of his rise to public acceptance he will be cunning and likable. He will be smart and have the ability to organize and move people.

According to the prophecy in Daniel, chapter 9, the Antichrist will come from the people who destroyed the temple which is Rome. Many Bible students believe that the Antichrist will emerge from the alliance of nations headquartered in the city of seven hills (Rev. 17). Traditionally the city of Rome has been called by the nickname of *the city of seven hills*. Even though the Roman Empire is gone, the final state of the Roman Empire as prophesied in Daniel two, has never been fulfilled. So, it is believed that the empire will be revived and be fulfilled during the end time. The beast is described as coming out of an alliance of ten horns (nations) and a smaller 11th horn will emerge from that alliance which will be the Antichrist. This alliance will be made up of ten kings from ten strong nations and could include many smaller countries, which do not have a strong government. Prophecy tells us that this 11th horn will uproot three of the kings (nations) when he rises to power (Daniel chapter 7). Who will make up this reconstructed Roman Empire? Many speculate that this could be the EU or even the UN or maybe a new alliance of nations.

Through the years many have thought that the Antichrist would come through the Catholic church because of its headquarters being located in Rome and the power and influence of the Pope. With the rise of Muslim presence and power in the world, especially in Europe, many speculate that it will be the source of uniting the world. A growing number believe that because the United States is not mentioned in prophecy that it could be one of these ten strong nations. Or it could be so closely aligned with Israel that she is seen we Israel.

The Antichrist will rise to power as he leads in signing a peace agreement ending the first war of Gog and Magog. He will rule from the city of Rome and his political system of government will be called Babylon. In the Bible, Babylon usually stands for a pagan, ungodly, and immoral government. He will gain control of the economy probably because of a world drought and lack of basic needs due to the first Gog and Magog war and God's judgment. He will set up a rationing system and require everyone to take his mark in order to purchase anything. It is easy to see how this could happen understanding the worldwide call for a global economy. We are fast moving towards a cashless society where cards are used instead of paper money. We have the technology to place chips with the owner's information under the skin of animals and in humans to record medical records. It is easy to see how the Antichrist's rationing system could be quickly implemented.

The Antichrist will become mad with his power. He takes control of the temple in Jerusalem and puts an image of himself in the Holy of Holies on the altar. The False Prophet will lead the world to serve the Antichrist as the Savior of the world. The Antichrist's ego will be so great that it will cause him to hate the witnesses of Christ and seek to destroy anyone who would worship God instead of him.

At the end of the battle of Armageddon the Antichrist and the False Prophet are thrown into the lake of fire for eternity.

F. **THE PERIOD OF TRIBULATION.** The Bible tells us that there is going to be a time of woes (Matt. 24:21; Rev. 7:14). The Bible seems clear that there will be a time of tribulation as judgment for the sin of the world. The worst of woes will last 3 1/2 years. Daniel 9:27 talks about a covenant made for one week by one who will cut off sacrifices in the middle of the week, which will escalate judgment and usher in the coming of Christ.

Daniel 9:27 (NKJV) Then he shall confirm a covenant with many for one week; But in the middle of the week He shall bring an end to sacrifice and offering. And on the wing of abominations shall be one who makes desolate, even until the consummation, which is determined, is poured out on the desolate."

Some people believe that Daniel 9:27 refers to the ministry of Christ. They say the Messiah was cut off in the midst of a week, or after 3 1/2 years of Jesus' earthly ministry. But that does not fit in Daniel's prophecy. Christ's earthly ministry was 3 1/2 years which is half of seven but it would seem difficult to say Christ ministry happened in half of its intended time frame. It does not fit to place the first coming of Jesus being interrupted by His return to heaven and then His coming back to rule as Messiah in a seven-year time frame.

Daniel 9:24 it says: 70 weeks are determined for the Jews and for the city of Jerusalem. The word "week" in Daniel's prophecy while accurate is unfortunate for our understanding. The Hebrew word "*Shabuwa*" found in the Hebrew text of Daniel 9:25 means "a period of seven". In context Daniel was referring to years so 70 groups of seven years would equal 490 years. God is saying that 490 years have been determined for Israel and in these 490 years God is going to fulfill all promises given to Israel. Some were fulfilled when Israel returned from Babylonian exile to Jerusalem. Some were fulfilled when Christ came the first time to be crucified and He rose again.

Here is how these 490 years breaks down. In verse 25 it says that the beginning of this 490 years was with the command to rebuild the city of Jerusalem. This command was given by Artaxerxes in 445 BC (Roman years were 360 days long instead of the 365 days like today which makes a difference in counting). This is 80 years after the decree to rebuild the Temple in Jerusalem. Continuing in verse 25 it tells us that after this decree there would be 7 x 7 weeks, which equals 49, and then 62 x 7 weeks which equal 483 years. Then in verse 26 it says that the Messiah will be cut off after this 483 years. Jesus was cut off at His crucifixion, which was in the year 33 AD. Then verse 26 goes on to say that the city and the temple would be destroyed which happened in 70 AD so this part of the prophecy ends in 70 AD.

Here is how we come up with seven years to be fulfilled: 445 BC to 32 AD (476 x 365 = 173,740 days). The amount of time between March 14 (when the decree was signed) until April 6 (the day of the triumphant entry) is 24 days. You figure in leap years and get 116 days. 172740 + 24 + 116 = 173,880 days or 483 years according to the lunar calendar recognized in that day. Seven years are left that have not been fulfilled when you subtract 483 years from 490 years.

When Israel rejected Christ as the Messiah, the Bible says (Rom. 11:25) that a partial hardening has happened to Israel until the fullness of the Gentiles has come. In other words, God is not dealing directly with Israel right now and won't be again until after the rapture of the church. This is a gap between the 483 years until after the rapture of the church when time starts again and the last seven years of dealing with Israel will begin.

Daniel 9:27 talks about "he" making an agreement for a week (seven years) and that "he" will break the agreement in the middle of the week stopping sacrifices in the temple. The "he" fits the Antichrist. According to Daniel 12:11 this happens after the abomination in the temple at the middle of the seven-year period. The last 3 1/2 years of tribulation will be known as the Great tribulation because the woes will greatly intensify.

Seeing seven years of tribulation beginning with a peace agreement being signed between the nations of the earth and Israel fits Daniel and Revelation prophecies. Signing the agreement fits at the end of the first war of Gog and Magog, which will begin the seven-year period of the tribulation.

G. **THE 144,000 WITNESSES.** Chapter 7 of Revelation tells us that after seeing six of the seals opened, John saw another angel having the seal of God. This angel shouted to the angels who were to carry out the seals to wait until the 144,000 witnesses were sealed before executing judgments. The witnesses were given the seal of God so that no harm could come upon them until their ministry had been completed.

Who are theses 144,000 witnesses? Nothing could be any clearer than the identity of these witnesses — they are all Jews. Chapter 7 of Revelation breaks down the number this way — 12,000 from each of the tribes of Israel. But the listing is different from the original list of tribes. In the Old Testament, the tribe of Levi was usually deleted from the list because they were the priestly tribe and were given portions of another tribe's land. Joseph's name was usually replaced by two of his sons, Ephraim and Manasseh, which kept the list at twelve.

In the list found in Revelation chapter 7, the tribes of Dan and Manasseh have been dropped and Levi and Joseph have been added. Why? Only God knows for sure, but the best guess is because Dan and Manasseh led Israel into idolatry. Because of that they will not be entrusted with sharing the gospel during the tribulation.

The list including Levi and Joseph (minus Ephraim and Manasseh) will be included on the twelve gates of the walls of New Jerusalem (Rev. 21:12). The wall around this future city was prophesied of in Ezekiel 48:30–34 where it says that they, the tribes of Israel, will be included in this significant recognition.

Why Jews? Remember that just before the tribulation begins, the church will be raptured. The church was God's witness on earth and she is gone. God's primary work is shifting from the church back to the Jews. These 144,000 Jews will witness and will help lead Jews to worship God and find the Messiah. They will be evangelists as well because Revelation 7:9 tells us many, many people of all nations will be saved as a result of their testimony.

How will they be chosen? We don't know, but that is not the focus. In some way Christ will reveal Himself to them and they will receive Him by faith. After the first battle of Gog and Magog that has just been miraculously won by God, we are told that Israel will see God's hand in this victory and will acknowledge Him. Perhaps this miracle will speak to these 144,000 in a way that they see Christ. Then we are told that an angel with God's seal will seal the 144,000 Jewish witnesses so that they cannot be killed and stopped from sharing the gospel until their ministry is completed.

These 144,000 Jews will be saved at the beginning of the tribulation to serve as God's witnesses on the earth after the witness of the church was taken away. Matthew 24 says that the gospel will be preached around the world and then the end will come. The 144,000 witnesses and then the two witnesses whose lives will be chronicled around the world on satellite TV will help to carry the gospel around the world.

H. **THE TWO WITNESSES.** Revelation 11:3 says that God will send two witnesses on the scene with miraculous powers. They will have the ability to defend themselves by breathing fire out of their mouths and destroying their enemies. They will have the power to turn water into blood and cause pestilence upon the land when they think it is necessary. People around the world will hate them seeing them as an enemy to the political system.

Who are they? Many believe they will be Moses and Elijah. They were both present at the transfiguration and the miracles that the two witnesses will perform will mirror what Elijah and Moses performed. Others think that they will be Elijah and Enoch because both were translated into heaven without facing physical death. One was a Gentile and the other a Jew that would correspond to the description in Revelation 11 of the two olive trees and the two lampstands. The olive tree being a picture of Israel and the lampstands the New Testament church. A strong argument for one of the witnesses being Elijah is found in:

Malachi 4:5 (NKJV) ⁵ Behold, I will send you Elijah the prophet before the coming of the great and dreadful day of the LORD.

While Elijah is a good candidate to be one of the witnesses, we are not told specifically who they are. The focus is not who they will be but rather the fact that God will send two witnesses to earth. Down to the last month of the earth as it is now, God will have a witness on earth proclaiming the good news of Jesus Christ and offering salvation to all who will repent and believe.

When do they show up? The best answer seems to be at the middle of the tribulation. We do know that the ministry of the two witnesses will last 1260 days which is about 18 days shy of 3 1/2 years. This would have the witnesses gone just days before the very end of time. The two witnesses will be sealed so that they can't be killed until their ministry is completed. They will have the ability to breathe fire from their mouths to consume anyone who tries to kill them (Rev. 11). They will have the power to stop the rain and cause a drought. They can turn water into blood and cause plagues they determine necessary to accomplish their ministry on earth.

When their ministry has been completed Satan will kill these two witnesses who are known to the world as enemies of the Antichrist. For 3 1/2 days the dead bodies will lay on a street in Jerusalem. The world will rejoice that the government's enemy has been killed. This will be the lead story on every news report around the world. While the world is watching and rejoicing, after 3 1/2 days of death the witnesses will jump up and stand tall in the street. The world will be terrified. Suddenly, a loud voice from heaven says, "come up here" and they ascend into heaven as the world watches. Immediately an earthquake occurs and destroys 1/10th of the city of Jerusalem. In the earthquake 7,000 people will be killed. The terrified survivors in the city give glory to God.

I. **REBUILDING OF THE TEMPLE.** Daniel 9:27; Daniel chapter 11; as well as Matthew 24 talk about the desecration of the temple. What does that mean? To desecrate, according to the Oxford dictionary, means to treat a sacred thing or place with violent disrespect or to violate it. Daniel prophesied that the temple would be desecrated. The temple was built by Solomon to be a permanent place for the ark of the covenant. Up until the dedication of the temple, the ark was stored in the tabernacle. The tabernacle was a movable tent that God instructed Israel to build when they came out of captivity in Egypt. This movable tabernacle was moved from place to place around Israel until this temple was constructed in Jerusalem giving it a permanent location.

The ark of the covenant represented God's presence with His people. That's why so much importance is given to the temple. It is hard to appreciate this importance because we, as New Testament believers, have the Holy Spirit as God's presence with us. The ark contained the original stone tablets that God had written the Ten Commandments on. The ark was placed in the Holy of Holies where only the high priest could enter and then only on certain occasions.

Where is the ark today? It appears that the ark was hidden in caves by the Priest when the city was invaded by Pharaoh Shishak of Egypt. King Josiah ordered that it be returned to the temple after danger had passed (2 Chron. 35:1–6). This is the last time the location of the ark is mentioned in the Old Testament.

Solomon's temple stood until it was destroyed by Babylon in 586 BCE, about 40 years after completion, on their 3rd invasion into Jerusalem. At that time, the valuable contents of the temple were taken and placed in the treasury of Babylon. Did they capture the ark of the covenant? No. Some believe that the ark was moved by priests into caves to protect it when it appeared that Babylon was going to invade them. Interestingly the ark of the covenant is mentioned in Revelation 11:19 as located in heaven. Some believe that God moved the ark into heaven for preservation. We know that the articles found in the Temple were copies of things in heaven. The ark that John saw was probably meant as a reminder that God has not forgotten Israel and that He is present with them. And as a reminder that temple worship will be restored. Zerubbabel led the first group of captives from Babylon back to Jerusalem and led them to rebuild the temple on the old site. It was consecrated in about 516 BC. This temple is called Zerubbabel's Temple.

In 20–19 BC Herod proposed to renovate the temple because, he said, when Zerubbabel rebuilt the temple it was 60 cubits shorter than Solomon's temple had been. It was completed in 63 AD. A courtyard, called the Court of the Gentiles, was added to allow Gentiles to worship. This renovated temple is referred to as Herod's Temple. Zerubbabel's temple was not exactly the same dimensions, and Herod's temple added the Court of the Gentiles, so neither was exactly like Solomon's Temple. This appears to be why John is instructed to measure the temple so that the temple rebuilt during the tribulation will be exactly like Solomon's temple.

Zerubbabel's temple was desecrated in 168 BC when the Syrian King Antiochus Epiphanes erected an image on the altar in the Holy of Holies and dedicated it to the pagan god Zeus. They then offered a pig on the altar. This desecrated the temple because worship in the temple dedicated to Jehovah God was redirected to the constructed image of Zeus. Epiphanes' millennial army offered a pig, which was unclean according to the dietary law given to the Jews, as a sacrifice on the altar. This desecration would only fulfill part of the prophecy because it did not bring on the end. Rome destroyed the temple in 70 AD.

In the same manner as Antiochus Epiphanes did, the Antichrist will build an image of himself and place it in the temple. When the image is built all worship and sacrifices to God will end. The temple is then desecrated and it becomes unclean. God will at this time bring great judgment upon the Antichrist, earth and evil by quickly sending great acts of judgment over the next 3 1/2 years bringing on the end of the world as we know it now.

There are several obstacles that need to be overcome before the temple can be rebuilt and sacrifice begun again. The Temple Institute in Israel declares that they have drawn up all of the architectural plans and have prefabricated many of the large sections of the Temple. The altar has been rebuilt so they can immediately begin to offer sacrifices after the Temple is complete. The Temple Institute has all of the priestly garments ready to be used by priests in the Temple.

There is an obstacle to it being rebuilt. No one is sure of the exact spot where the Holy of Holies (in the second temple) was located on the Temple Mount. Where it is thought to have been located is where the Al-Aqsa Mosque is standing today. When the war of Psalm 83 is fought, and won, that will give control of this site to Israel. It easily could be built before the midpoint when the temple is desecrated.

Another problem is that the Jews today are ritually impure which prevents them from entering the spot where temple stood. To become ritually pure, they would need the ashes of a pure Red Angus Heifer

(Num. 19:1–6) and a priest who can trace his lineage back far enough to validate his claim to be of the priestly line to administer ashes of Red Heifer.

A three-year old cow with pure red hair, absolutely no other color hair on the cow, was found several years ago. More than $100,000 has been raised for the breeding of a pure red heifer worthy to be burnt and her ashes used to purify the priest so they can offer sacrifices. When the temple is rebuilt in Jerusalem, the synagogue will revert back to temple worship and the Rabbis will revert to the work of the Priest.

J. **THE NEW CITY OF JERUSALEM.** What is the New City of Jerusalem? The New Jerusalem is also called the Tabernacle of God, the Holy City, the City of God, the Celestial City, the City Foursquare, and Heavenly Jerusalem. It will literally be heaven on earth. It is referred to in the Bible in several places, but it is most fully described in Gal. 4:26.

The New City of Jerusalem actually is being prepared in heaven now. Jesus told His Apostles that there are many mansions in His Father's House and that He was going to prepare a place for them, the New Testament believers. Jesus went on to say that as He goes to prepare this place He will come again and receive them, the church, in the air and carry them to heaven (John 14 1:1–4). While this city is built for Christ's bride (Rev. 22:3), the New Testament church, it will become the center for all believers during the millennial kingdom. The city will be the capital of the new earth where Christ and His bride will rule over Israel.

When Jesus speaks at the battle of Armageddon it will destroy the Antichrist, his political system, and all the kings and armies of the earth. God is then going to remake the earth and the atmosphere above it (Rev. 21:1; Is. 65:17; 2 Peter 3:12–13). After this re-creation the City will descend from heaven to the spot where old Jerusalem had stood. The city is described as a bride beautifully dressed for her husband (Rev. 21:2). This is the city that Abraham looked for in faith (Heb.11:10).

The city is described as 1400 miles long x 1400 miles wide x 1400 miles high (Rev. 21: 15–17). It will stand on twelve layers of foundation with the name of one of the Apostles on each. Why the Apostles names on the foundation? We are not told, but it could be because it was the ministry of the Apostles that set the foundation for the New Testament church. The foundations are layered will all kinds of beautiful and precious stones (Rev. 21:19). It will have three gates on each of the four walls. These twelve gates will each be made from one large pearl. A name of an individual tribe of Israel will be inscribed on each of the twelve gates.

This city will have an individual space, a mansion as the KJV describes it, for every believer. It will be moved from God's heaven to the earth after the earth has been cleansed by fire. The gold street with twelve trees of life growing along the river of life flow from the throne of Jesus Christ.

K. **THE MARRIAGE FEAST.** In Revelation 19:7–10 John saw and heard songs of jubilation because the Marriage Feast of the Lamb was about to begin. To understand better the marriage feast it helps to understand the Jewish wedding customs during the time of Christ.

The wedding customs had three major steps. First, the father of the groom and the father of the bride signed a marriage contract. The bridegroom, or his father, would pay a dowry to the bride or her parents. This step was called the betrothal period—what today is called the engagement. This step was the one Joseph and Mary were in when she was told that she was pregnant.

The second step usually occurred around a year later. The groom, accompanied by his male friends, would go to the house of the bride late at night carrying torches, which appeared like a parade through the streets. The bride would know that the groom would be coming in about a year. While the bride does not know the exact time, she and her maidens would be ready and watching around this time. The male friends of the bridegroom would go ahead of the groom as they approached the bride's house and sound a trumpet to announce the grooms approach. The bride and her attendants would come out of the house and all would join the parade, which ended up at the groom's father's house where the marriage ceremony was performed.

After the wedding ceremony the groom and his bride enter a chamber built for the couple to consummate the marriage. While the couple is in the chamber, all of the guests wait outside until the groom came out and announced that the consummation was complete and offer proof that the bride was a virgin. Then the feast would begin.

The third step was the marriage feast itself which lasted for days (usually seven). This is illustrated by the wedding at Cana. What John sees in Revelation 19 is the wedding feast of the Lamb (Jesus Christ) and His Bride (the church), which is this third step. So it is implied that the first two steps have already taken place.

The first step (signing of the contract) was completed when each individual believer places their faith in Christ. The dowry paid is the blood of Christ. The church on earth today is "betrothed" to Christ and, like the wise virgins in the parable, all believers should be watching and waiting for the appearance of the Groom (the). The second phase symbolizes the rapture of the church when Christ comes to claim His bride and take her to His Father's house.

The Marriage Feast then follows as the third and final step. When will the Marriage Feast take place? If the ancient Jewish custom were a guide it would take place after the wedding ceremony and consummation. At the rapture the church has been given her heavenly body and dressed with a white robe proving her virginity. The Bema seat judgment has happened and the bride will have received her rewards for obedience. Then the wedding ceremony takes place. Perhaps the bride will then present her rewards to her husband as an act of love, the consummation. All of this seems to happen in a matter of a very short time. Then the marriage feast will begin and last while the seven years of tribulation is happening on the earth.

There will be others attending the wedding feast besides the bride of Christ the church. The "others" include the Old Testament saints. We are not told that they have received their robes of white and their heavenly bodies yet. But their souls/spirits went to heaven when they died so they will be present. Perhaps these Old Testament saints and the church are given temporary bodies before they receive their heavenly bodies. The church will be given their heavenly body at the rapture and Old Testament saints along with tribulation saints will receive theirs after the millennial kingdom is over as they go into eternity. As the angel told John to write, "Blessed are those who are invited to the marriage supper of the Lamb" The marriage supper of the Lamb will be a glorious celebration of all who are in Christ!

While there is disagreement about the exact placement of these events on God's timeline there should be no disagreement about the fact that they will happen.

L. **THE MILLENNIAL KINGDOM.** Some say that this is not a literal reign of Christ on earth sighting the thousand years as an allegory meaning a long time. However, Revelation 20 mentions six times that it is 1,000 years long. After Armageddon the earth will be cleansed by fire and all of the effects of the curse of sin will be gone. It will be a perfect environment spiritually and physically. Because only believers will be in the Kingdom there will be complete obedience to God. John saw the new heaven and earth before the city was set down and it had no sea so the land was contiguous (Rev. 21). All of the Old Testament and tribulation saints will inhabit the land outside of Jerusalem but will have complete access into Jerusalem and fellowship with the Savior. Christ will bring His bride, the New Testament church, to her city and tribulation saints will inhabit the land of Israel around its capital city Jerusalem. Chapter 2 of Isaiah describes this new kingdom by saying all of the swords will be beaten into plowshares and spears into pruning hooks. There will be absolute peace in this new kingdom because all of sins curse on man and the earth have been removed.

Revelation 20:6 (NKJV) [6] Blessed and holy *is* he who has part in the first resurrection. Over such the second death has no power, but they shall be priests of God and of Christ, and shall reign with Him a thousand years.

What is the difference between the first resurrection and the second? Daniel 12:2 describes two different fates that mankind will face and they are drastically different. One happens at the first resurrection and the other fate happens at the second resurrection. Daniel 12:2 (ESV) says: "And many of those who sleep in the dust of the earth shall awake, some to everlasting life, and some to shame and everlasting contempt."

Revelation 20:4 – 6 talks about a first resurrection and who that those who are involved are blessed and holy and that the lake of fire has no power over them. The first resurrection takes place using several stages. Jesus was the first fruit of this resurrection. In Matthew 27 it tells us of a resurrection of Jerusalem saints. We are awaiting the resurrection we refer to as the rapture of the church. Those saved during the tribulation and killed will go to heaven where the Old Testament Saints await new bodies and those saved and alive at the end of the Tribulation will be have the curse of sin removed from their bodies and move into Israel for the Millennial Kingdom. At the end of the Millennial Kingdom Old Testament and Tribulation saints will get their glorified bodies. The first rapture refers to all who have trusted Jesus Christ as their personal Savior.

Where are the souls of people of the first resurrection? In heaven. When Old Testament saints died, immediately their souls went to heaven. When church saints die their souls immediately go to heaven awaiting the resurrection of saints who are still alive. John saw the souls of those who had been martyred during the tribulation under the altar in heaven meaning they were in God's protection but not in glorified bodies yet. The church saints receive their glorified bodies at the rapture.

Revelation 20 tells us that those of the second resurrection are identified as those who are judged because of their sin and cast into the lake of fire. After 1,000 years of Christ ruling over Israel in New Jerusalem, Satan will be released and he will raise an army. Who will this army be? The unsaved of earth will be killed during Armageddon. Many tribulation saints will have been martyred and others have died and they will be in heaven with God. All of the tribulation saints who survived the tribulation will enter the millennial kingdom. After Armageddon the earth will be cleansed from the curse of sin so no sinner could live on earth. So who will these nations be that Satan will gather when he is loosed from the bottomless pit?

While no one knows for sure, Revelation 20:9 says that they will be gathered from the four corners of the world. This means that they come from the earth and not from the bottomless pit. Because only saints will be on earth and they have eternal security, they won't be deceived by Satan. We are not told where they will come from but one of the best guesses seems to be from children born to these tribulation saints. They have been given bodies freed from the curse of sin but not their heavenly bodies, which they will receive after the millennial kingdom when they enter eternity. Children born in this "Garden of Eden" atmosphere have never been tempted to sin until Satan is released. Then they must choose obedience to Christ or Satan.

While we don't know the details of who Satan's army will be, we do know Satan will engage in a battle against Christ during the second war of Gog and Magog. Satan will be quickly defeated and then will be cast into the lake of fire for eternity.

M. **THE GREAT WHITE THRONE JUDGMENT.** This judgment is described in Revelation 20. It will happen after the millennial kingdom is over and Satan is cast into the lake of fire. Every lost person from every age along with those who participated in the rebellion by Satan will be called from the place of death to stand before the White Throne of God. The place of death, Shoal, or Hades, is the place where the lost go when they die. The exact location of the place of death is not known but is probably in another part of hell separate from the bottomless pit or their final destination the lake of fire.

Revelation 20 tells us the books along with the Book of Life are opened. What are the books? We are not told. Some believe that the books contain all the sins of life which would show that everyone at this judgment have unpaid sin and if their name is not written in the Lamb's book of Life, they will receive the wages of their sin — eternal spiritual death.

Still others believe that the books contain the law of God, which is God's standard of righteousness. Anyone who had violated God's law (which is everyone), if their name is not found in the Lamb's Book of Life they will be cast into the lake of fire.

The books might be either one or both or something else. What the books are is not the focus. The focus is that this judgment is fair and just because everyone cast into the lake of fire will be there because they chose not to accept Christ's offer of life. They deserve to be cast into the lake of fire as a payment for their sin.

N. **ETERNITY.** After the millennial kingdom is over and the Great White Throne Judgment has been completed, then all of the saved will be ushered into eternity. Where will saints spend eternity? In heaven with God forever. Some believe that will be in the New Heaven on earth where the New City of Jerusalem has been set. Others believe the New City of Jerusalem will be carried into God's heaven. Either way, the focus is clear that the saints will live in heaven with God forever.

THE BOOK OF REVELATION

1. BACKGROUND OF THE BOOK OF REVELATION.

Jesus gave His revelation to a man named John and instructed him to accurately record all that he saw. Who was John? He was the son of Zebedee and Salome. John had a brother, also an apostle, named James (not Jesus' half-brother, another apostle named James). John and James were called "Sons of Thunder" which described their gentle loving nature until their patience was pushed to its limits. Then they became wild and thunderous speaking out like a storm. A story relates how the brothers wanted to call down fire on a town, but Jesus rebuked them. John lived more than fifty years after the martyrdom of his brother James, who tradition says was the first apostle to die a martyr's death.

It was John to whom Jesus gave the responsibility of taking care of Mary, His mother, even though Mary had several other children. This shows the trust that Jesus had in John. Tradition tells us that John brought Mary to his house and cared for all of her needs for the rest of her life.

John wrote the gospel of John as well as First, Second, and Third John, and Revelation. John was about 90 years old when he wrote the book of Revelation.

The Bible tells us that John was sentenced to a small Greek island named Patmos. Patmos, a quarry mine for the Roman Empire, was located in the Aegean Sea. It was used to house political and religious prisoners of Rome. Tradition says that the ruler Domitian got angry with John because he didn't die when he was dipped in hot oil, so he banished him to the island of Patmos. If John's body was burned with hot oil, can't you image the daily pain he suffered? Yet, his faith was unwavering.

John was on this populated island as a prisoner when Jesus gave him the book of Revelation. John wrote down what he saw. Just imagine what it must have been like as John saw these things from the future. He was miraculously transported from the primitive, non-technical age of the first century into the future. John witnesses the most horrific war of all times, fought with weapons completely beyond his comprehension.

SUMMARY OF INTRODUCTION: So John, an old man imprisoned for boldly preaching the gospel, is on an island that was used as a penal colony. John, a prisoner on an island that was a Roman quarry mine probably had to work in the mine for the government. One day this seasoned saint, who had witnessed the murder of many of his friends because of their faith, was given a vision of a time when all of the injustice and evil of this world would be judged. This judgment will usher in a place where true believers will live with Jesus Christ in an absolute righteous environment. What a blessing!

Remember as you study the book of Revelation not to totally focus on the symbolism. When it becomes the main focus, it can overshadow the message. Discussion about what these symbols mean can be productive but they are not the focus. These graphic symbols describe how intense the judgments will be.

CHAPTER 1

Revelation Chapter 1

Verses 1 through 8 give an introduction to the book of Revelation. Verses 1 through 3 establish the setting and background details that set the stage for the coming prophecy.

Revelation 1: (NKJV)

¹ The Revelation of Jesus Christ, which God gave Him to show His servants — things which must shortly take place. And He sent and signified it by His angel to His servant John,

Clearly John is not the one revealing. Jesus Christ is revealing to John things that will happen in the future. Seeing the future reminds us that God is in control of time. Verse 1 tells us things must shortly take place and many years have passed since then and the end hasn't come yet. That doesn't mean the Bible was wrong and these things won't happen. The Bible tells us that to God one year is like a thousand years. In other words, God doesn't mark time like we do because He is eternal. A couple thousand years will be a short time to God, and these things will happen just like He said (2 Peter 3:8, Ps. 90:4).

² who bore witness to the word of God, and to the testimony of Jesus Christ, to all things that he saw. ³ Blessed *is* he who reads and those who hear the words of this prophecy, and keep those things which are written in it; for the time *is* near.

Here is a promise of blessing to the person who reads the book of Revelation and really hears what it is saying. Then he says that it is more than just reading and understanding the book, it is practicing the message found in the book as well. How do you practice prophecy? When you believe by faith the promises found in Revelation it gives you strength and comfort. By knowing the prophecies will be fulfilled just exactly as it has been given, we know God is going to judge life's injustices, reward obedience, and give eternal life to all who truly believe. Remember that God knows what's going on and He is working His plan in His time.

⁴ John, to the seven churches which are in Asia: Grace to you and peace from Him who is and who was and who is to come, and from the seven Spirits who are before His throne,

John needs no introduction to these churches. He had ministered in this area for many years and his reputation was known and respected. John sent copies of this book, including all of the letters, probably by messenger to each church. It was the custom of churches of this day to copy letters from apostles like John and pass them along to other churches. They did this because they did not have the compiled Bible like we do. These letters contain admonition and warnings to churches of all time.

⁵ and from Jesus Christ, the faithful witness, the firstborn from the dead, and the ruler over the kings of the earth. To Him who loved us and washed us from our sins in His own blood, ⁶ and has made us kings and priests to His God and Father, to Him be glory and dominion forever and ever. Amen.

John identifies the revelator of this book as the one who had power over death. Because of His perfect life and shed blood He paid the price for our sin debt. Of course this is Jesus Christ.

⁷ Behold, He is coming with clouds, and every eye will see Him, even they who pierced Him. And all the tribes of the earth will mourn because of Him. Even so, Amen. ⁸ "I am the Alpha and the Omega, *the* Beginning and *the* End," says the Lord, "who is and who was and who is to come, the Almighty."

John gives us a preview of coming events. At the second coming of Jesus Christ, which happens at the end of the Tribulation period, everyone will recognize who Jesus is. When they recognize Jesus the world mourns because of their sinful condition. This is not repentance for salvation because by this time it is too late. Then Christ will speak and defeat the evil world at the Battle of Armageddon. The everlasting God is coming to bring judgment for sin, claim ownership of the earth, and set up His earthly kingdom.

⁹ I, John, both your brother and companion in the tribulation and kingdom and patience of Jesus Christ, was on the island that is called Patmos for the word of God and for the testimony of Jesus Christ.

John identifies that in God's timing he had suffered trials and tribulations as a believer. He was imprisoned for preaching the gospel of Jesus Christ. John declares that he will join all believers in the coming kingdom.

¹⁰ I was in the Spirit on the Lord's Day, and I heard behind me a loud voice, as of a trumpet, ¹¹ saying, "I am the Alpha and the Omega, the First and the Last," and, "What you see, write in a book and send *it* to the seven churches which are in Asia: to Ephesus, to Smyrna, to Pergamos, to Thyatira, to Sardis, to Philadelphia and to Laodicea." ¹² Then I turned to see the voice that spoke with me. And having turned I saw seven golden lampstands, ¹³ and in the midst of the seven lampstands *One* like the Son of Man, clothed with a garment down to the feet and girded about the chest with a golden band. ¹⁴ His head and hair *were* white like wool, as white as snow, and His eyes like a flame of fire; ¹⁵ His feet *were* like fine brass, as if refined in a furnace, and His voice as the sound of many waters; ¹⁶ He had in His right hand seven stars, out of His mouth went a sharp two-edged sword, and His countenance *was* like the sun shining in its strength. ¹⁷ And when I saw Him, I fell at His feet as dead. But He laid His right hand on me, saying to me, "Do not be afraid; I am the First and the Last. ¹⁸ I *am* He who lives, and was dead, and behold, I am alive forevermore. Amen. And I have the keys of Hades and of Death. ¹⁹ Write the things which you have seen, and the things which are, and the things which will take place after this. ²⁰ The mystery of the seven stars which you saw in My right hand, and the seven golden lampstands: The seven stars are the angels of the seven churches, and the seven lampstands which you saw are the seven churches.

On a Sunday, as John was totally focused on the Holy Spirit, Jesus begins to show him things to record in a book. After John finished recording what was revealed to him he was told to send it to seven of the churches located in Asia. John saw seven lampstands which represented these churches and he saw Jesus walking in and around them. Jesus had in His right hand their pastors and gives to them the Word of God. Jesus reminds John that He overcame death and now holds the keys to the eternal destiny of man.

SUMMARY. The main message of chapter 1 is that the book of Revelation was given by Jesus under the authority of God the Father and everything in it is accurate. The message can be believed because of the ability of the One who is revealing the message. God has a plan and He is working His plan in His time. Jesus is present in His churches today like He was in John's day and Christ is aware of everything going on in them. Jesus gives His authority to faithful preachers to boldly preach His mighty Word.

CHAPTER 2

Revelation Chapters 2 and 3

TIMELINE: These letters were written somewhere between 86 & 91 AD to churches located on or near prime trade routes in Asia. Most of these churches were located in what we know as Turkey today. These letters recorded by John addressed complaints and admonition of practices found in each church. While they were sent to these churches in the first century the message in these letters should speak to churches until the church age is over (at the rapture).

Being located on or near a prime trade route is significant because there were many foreigners who traveled through these cities to other locations around the region. Jesus told John to carefully write all that he would see in a book and include these letters in it. Then he was to send copies of the book to the seven churches and the churches could make copies and send them by way of believing visitors to many places around the region. This is one of the ways God used to preserve and spread the teaching of this important book.

Chapter 2:1–7
John writes a letter to the church located in Ephesus.
The city of Ephesus had Greek and Roman cultures which color the lifestyle of the city. History tells us that children at the age of seven would start school where they would learn history, music, logics, astronomy, Greek language, poetry and units of measurement. This tells us they placed a premium on education. Their worship tradition was of sacrificing animals to pagan gods and goddesses. There was a famous temple here for the Goddess Artemis.

Many here believed in reincarnation. The port city of Ephesus was prosperous and citizens were typically wealthy. The Romans enjoyed eating and drinking and having parties in the public bathhouses. It is believed that John brought Mary, Jesus' mother, to live out her life here.

Revelation 2:1–7 (NKJV) ¹"To the angel of the church of Ephesus write, 'These things says He who holds the seven stars in His right hand, who walks in the midst of the seven golden lampstands: ² I know your works, your labor, your patience, and that you cannot bear those who are evil. And you have tested those who say they are apostles and are not, and have found them liars; ³ and you have persevered and have patience, and have labored for My name's sake and have not become weary. ⁴ Nevertheless I have *this* against you, that you have left your first love. ⁵ Remember therefore from where you have fallen; repent and do the first works, or else I will come to you quickly and remove your lampstand from its place — unless you repent. ⁶ But this you have, that you hate the deeds of the Nicolaitans, which I also hate. ⁷ He who has an ear, let him hear what the Spirit says to the churches. To him who overcomes I will give to eat from the tree of life, which is in the midst of the Paradise of God."

Here is a paraphrased copy of this letter.

Dear Pastor of the church located in Ephesus,

Jesus, who is holding your church in His right hand and is working all around you, has some observations about the ministry of your church.

I see all that you are doing and I recognize how patiently you have worked for Me. You have little tolerance for those who do evil things. You are very careful to make sure that anyone who comes in My name, really has a message that has been authorized by Me. You are working hard for my kingdom. I know that you have found many who claimed to be sent by Me but wanted to spread false doctrine. I know that you have not gotten discouraged by all your work or by those who sought to deceive you.

However, there is something that bothers Me. You are working hard but you have lost your motivation of doing it because you love Me. You are going through the motions, but have lost sight of the vision that you once had. Stop and think about how you once served with joy and a sense of mission. Ask forgiveness for moving so far from Me and come back by My side. If you don't, I will remove My blessings from you. I do recognize how you hate the teaching that works of the flesh have no effect on your spiritual life; I hate that teaching as well. Let everyone hear what this letter says. Remember, everyone who has saving faith in Me will have everlasting life with Me in Paradise.

Love,
Jesus Christ

Chapter 2:8-11
John writes a letter to the church located in Smyrna.

Smyrna was a large seaport city located about 35 miles north of Ephesus. Many believed it to be the most beautiful city of the seven cities that Jesus sent letters to. Its streets were wide and paved. It had its own system of coinage and was recognized for its schools of science and medicine and for the beautiful architecture. This was an advanced society in education and social structure. The economy in Smyrna was very good because of its industry and being located on a trade route. The citizens in Smyrna exhibited great patriotism to the Roman government and had great pride in their city. There were many Jews who lived in Smyrna and had great influence. These Jews did all they could to hurt the church and make it difficult for believers to find good jobs.

[8] "And to the angel of the church in Smyrna write, 'These things says the First and the Last, who was dead, and came to life: [9] I know your works, tribulation, and poverty (but you are rich); and *I know* the blasphemy of those who say they are Jews and are not, but *are* a synagogue of Satan. [10] Do not fear any of those things which you are about to suffer. Indeed, the devil is about to throw *some* of you into prison, that you may be tested, and you will have tribulation ten days. Be faithful until death, and I will give you the crown of life. [11] He who has an ear, let him hear what the Spirit says to the churches. He who overcomes shall not be hurt by the second death."'

Here is a paraphrased copy of this letter.
Dear Pastor of the church located in Smyrna,

As your eternal Savior, I know what you have done and of your tribulations. Even though you don't have much materially you are really very wealthy. I have heard the hurtful things that people, who say they are Jews, but really are workers of Satan, are saying. Trouble is coming upon you but take comfort. Some of you will be thrown into prison and others will face many problems. Stay faithful as long as you live and I will give you everlasting life. Let everyone hear what this letter says. Remember everyone who has a saving faith in Me will never face spiritual death and separation from Me.

Love,
Jesus Christ

Chapter 2:12–17
John writes a letter to the church located in Pergamos.

The city of Pergamos was on top of a mountain along the Turkish coastline overlooking the Aegean Sea. It was known for its scientific advancements in the field of medicine. It's location along both land and sea-trading routes made it a prosperous city. People would come from all over the Mediterranean region to find good jobs or to receive medical treatments. There was a great library which had an estimated 40,000 volumes housed within its walls. The Hellenistic culture, which is a culture that indulges in philosophy and logic, can be seen in its remains. Antipas, a Christian bishop, was believed to have been martyred here which may be a part of the reason that John calls it the place where Satan dwells. Satan has tremendous influence in this city.

¹² "And to the angel of the church in Pergamos write, 'These things says He who has the sharp two-edged sword: ¹³ I know your works, and where you dwell, where Satan's throne *is*. And you hold fast to My name, and did not deny My faith even in the days in which Antipas *was* My faithful martyr, who was killed among you, where Satan dwells.

¹⁴ But I have a few things against you, because you have there those

who hold the doctrine of Balaam, who taught Balak to put a stumbling block before the children of Israel, to eat things sacrificed to idols, and to commit sexual immorality. ¹⁵ Thus you also have those who hold the doctrine of the Nicolaitans, which thing I hate. ¹⁶ Repent, or else I will come to you quickly and will fight against them with the sword of My mouth.

¹⁷ He who has an ear, let him hear what the Spirit says to the churches. To him who overcomes I will give some of the hidden manna to eat. And I will give him a white stone, and on the stone a new name written which no one knows except him who receives *it*."

Here is a paraphrased copy of this letter.

Dear Pastor of the church located in Pergamos,

The one who gave the convicting Word of God is writing to you. I know your works and that you have not denied Me. You have remained faithful even though you live in a society that is evil. You have remained faithful even after Antipas, whom you knew well, was tortured and killed for faithfully serving Me.

However, I have some complaints against you. You have allowed many to serve in your church who were motivated by money rather than their love for Me. These false teachers have perverted the message of the Gospel in order to keep money coming into the church. Just like Balak did when he took money to put a curse on God's people. They are teaching that it is all right to eat the meat that has been offered to false gods while God said not to eat of it. They also are teaching that perverse sexual acts in the name of worship are good but it is a sin.

Not only that, you are allowing people to teach in your church who teach that the pursuit of worldly things won't affect your spiritual life. This I really hate. If you are broken-hearted because you have failed in your service to Me, then stop allowing these doctrines in your church. If you don't, then My Word will create divisions and conflicts in your fellowship.

Believers listen to what My Spirit is saying to you. I will give spiritual food that is hidden from you now to those who have saving faith. And I will give you a white stone with your new name on it. It is a name that no one else knows.

Love,
Jesus Christ

Chapter 2:12–17
John writes a letter to the church located in Thyatira.
The city of Thyatira is the smallest of the seven cities. It was located about 45 miles southeast of Pergamum and was famous for its textiles. Especially known for purple dye and for its powerful trade guilds. This city was not as prominent as the previous cities in that it was not as strategically located on a trade route. The trade guilds were very organized. Some of the most prominent of guilds were the coppersmiths and dyers of purple cloth. Pagan feasts with immoral practices seem to have been associated with the guilds. These guilds were so powerful that a person had to be a practicing member to hold a good job. These guilds were opposed to the Christians because of their teaching against their immoral practices.

[18] "And to the angel of the church in Thyatira write, 'These things says the Son of God, who has eyes like a flame of fire, and His feet like fine brass: [19] I know your works, love, service, faith, and your patience; and *as* for your works, the last *are* more than the first. [20] Nevertheless I have a few things against you, because you allow that woman Jezebel, who calls herself a prophetess, to teach and seduce My servants to commit sexual immorality and eat things sacrificed to idols. [21] And I gave her time to repent of her sexual immorality, and she did not repent. [22] Indeed I will cast her into a sickbed, and those who commit adultery with her into great tribulation, unless they repent of their deeds. [23] I will kill her children with death, and all the churches shall know that I am He who searches the minds and hearts. And I will give to each one of you according to your works. [24] Now to you I say, and to the rest in Thyatira, as many as do not have this doctrine, who have not known the depths of Satan, as they say, I will put on you no other burden. [25] But hold fast

what you have till I come. ²⁶ And he who overcomes, and keeps My works until the end, to him I will give power over the nations — ²⁷ *'He shall rule them with a rod of iron; They shall be dashed to pieces like the potter's vessels'* — as I also have received from My Father; ²⁸ and I will give him the morning star. ²⁹ He who has an ear, let him hear what the Spirit says to the churches."

Here is a paraphrased copy of this letter.

Dear Pastor of the church located in Thyatira,

These are the absolute and unchanging words of Jesus Christ who has eyes that can see your true motives. I know all that you are doing and that you are faithfully serving in love with perseverance. I know that you are now doing even more for Me than you did at first.

But I have this against you. You tolerate a woman who professes to be a prophetess, but she is not. She is teaching that sexual immorality is proper in your worship and that eating meats previously offered to false gods is all right even though it associates you with a pagan religion.

In My love I have given her the time necessary to repent, but she refuses. So, I am going to send pain and suffering upon her and all who keep following her teachings and do not repent.

To the rest of you in the church who are not following these teachings of Satan, I will not inflict you with pain. But I charge you to continue in My teachings until I come again.

To those who have saving faith I will give you authority over the nations, just like My Father has given Me authority. You will rule with the One who rules with iron and will smash into pieces the unrighteous just like a broken ceramic bowl. Because of your saving faith, you will personally be received into My presence.

Let everyone hear what this letter says.

Love,
Jesus Christ

Chapter 3:1–6
John writes a letter to the church located in Sardis.

Sardis was located on a hill about 30 miles south of Thyatira. This hill had walls on three sides and could only be approached from the south via a steep path. This seemingly impregnable city became overconfident and on two occasions they let their guard down and were defeated.

Revelation 3 (NKJV) [1] "And to the angel of the church in Sardis write, 'These things says He who has the seven Spirits of God and the seven stars: "I know your works, that you have a name that you are alive, but you are dead. [2] Be watchful, and strengthen the things which remain, that are ready to die, for I have not found your works perfect before God. [3] Remember therefore how you have received and heard; hold fast and repent. Therefore if you will not watch, I will come upon you as a thief, and you will not know what hour I will come upon you. [4] You have a few names even in Sardis who have not defiled their garments; and they shall walk with Me in white, for they are worthy. [5] He who overcomes shall be clothed in white garments, and I will not blot out his name from the Book of Life; but I will confess his name before My Father and before His angels. [6] He who has an ear, let him hear what the Spirit says to the churches."

Here is a paraphrased copy of this letter.

Dear Pastor of the church located in Sardis,

This letter is from Jesus who has the knowledge of the Holy Spirit and holds your church in His hand. He knows everything that you are doing and why you do it. You have a reputation of being spiritually dead. Be aware of your condition before the only spiritual life you have left dies. Remember what you have been taught — repent and become obedient to God's teachings. If you don't, I will come quietly without warning. I will identify with the few people In Sardis who are still faithful to Me. To those who have saving faith in Me, I will give entrance into heaven and announce them to My Father and His angels.

Let everyone hear what this letter says.

Love,
Jesus Christ

Chapter 3:7–13
John writes a letter to the church located in Philadelphia.
The city of Philadelphia was located 27 miles from Sardis and 48 miles from Laodicea. On one side of the city they grew grapes and was known for their fine wine. There were many pagan temples in the city.

[7] "And to the angel of the church in Philadelphia write, 'These things says He who is holy, He who is true, *"He who has the key of David, He who opens and no one shuts, and shuts and no one opens"*. [8] I know your works. See, I have set before you an open door, and no one can shut it; for you have a little strength, have kept My word, and have not denied My name. [9] Indeed I will make *those* of the synagogue of Satan, who say they are Jews and are not, but lie — indeed I will make them come and worship before your feet, and to know that I have loved you. [10] Because you have kept My command to persevere, I also will keep you from the hour of trial which shall come upon the whole world, to test those who dwell on the earth. [11] Behold, I am coming quickly! Hold fast what you have, that no one may take your crown. [12] He who overcomes, I will make him a pillar in the temple of My God, and he shall go out no more. And I will write on him the name of My God and the name of the city of My God, the New Jerusalem, which comes down out of heaven from My God. And *I will write on him* My new name. [13] He who has an ear, let him hear what the Spirit says to the churches."

Here is a paraphrased copy of this letter.
Dear Pastor of the church located in Philadelphia,
   This is the word of the Holy and True Lord who holds the key of life and death. I have the power to open and close what men can't. I know what you are doing so I have opened a door of opportunity that man cannot close. You are weak in your physical strength. But in your spiritual strength you are strong because you have been obedient to my Word and are not ashamed of My name.
   I will make those who lie about being Jews see that I have given you an open door because of your faith. One day you will abide with Me and these that persecute you now will then bow down and receive their judgment. Because of your saving faith in Me I will keep

you from great tribulations that in the future will fall upon the earth because of sin. Remember I will return to the earth soon so remain faithful.

To those with saving faith I will bring you into My presence eternally. I will give you an identity in Me by giving You a new family name, My name.

Let everyone hear what this letter says.

Love,
Jesus Christ

Chapter 3:14–22
John writes a letter to the church located in Laodicea.

The city of Laodicea is located just a few miles to the west of Colossae. It was a large and very important city. It was a city that became a center of industry especially known for its fine black wool and a powder used as medicine for the eyes. These industries made it wealthy. Laodicea was a leading banking center. Water was a big issue in the city. It had to get water from surrounding cities that ran in aqua ducts under the ground. By the time it got to Laodicea it was dirty and tepid. If you weren't used to the foul taste when you drank it you would naturally spit it out of your mouth. Jesus use of spewing the church out of his mouth was easily understood by the Laodicean reader.

¹⁴ "And to the angel of the church of the Laodiceans write, 'These things says the Amen, the Faithful and True Witness, the Beginning of the creation of God: ¹⁵ I know your works, that you are neither cold nor hot. I could wish you were cold or hot. ¹⁶ So then, because you are lukewarm, and neither cold nor hot, I will vomit you out of My mouth. ¹⁷ Because you say, 'I am rich, have become wealthy, and have need of nothing' — and do not know that you are wretched, miserable, poor, blind, and naked — ¹⁸ I counsel you to buy from Me gold refined in the fire, that you may be rich; and white garments, that you may be clothed, *that* the shame of your nakedness may not be revealed; and anoint your eyes with eye salve, that you may see. ¹⁹ As many as I love, I rebuke and chasten. Therefore be zealous and repent. ²⁰ Behold, I stand at the door and knock. If anyone hears My voice and opens the door, I will come

in to him and dine with him, and he with Me. ²¹ To him who overcomes I will grant to sit with Me on My throne, as I also overcame and sat down with My Father on His throne. ²² He who has an ear, let him hear what the Spirit says to the churches."

Here is a paraphrased copy of this letter.
Dear Pastor of the church located in Laodicea,

I know what you do and while you are not openly against Me, you don't have the proper desire to serve Me either. I wish you had a desire to know and serve Me. I wish you had saving faith in Me. Because you don't have saving faith in Me I will keep you from entering heaven.

You have a lot of material things and you think that you are doing well but in reality you are poor and miserable. If you want genuine wealth accept My offer of salvation so that your eyes will be opened to see what really matters.

Because I love my children I will discipline them and give those who are not Mine an opportunity to be adopted by My Father through saving faith in Me. As the Holy Spirit convicts the unbelievers heart if they will accept My invitation I will give to them a place in eternity with the Father and the Son and the Holy Spirit forever.

Let everyone hear what this letter says.

Love,
Jesus Christ

SUMMARY: Jesus said in these letters that the church was to be very careful to maintain true doctrine. So, they must always be on guard that teachers don't come in and begin to teach false doctrine. They must beware not to bring the pagan traditions of society into the church and incorporate them in worship. The church must be careful not to lose her vision and proper motivation for serving Christ. Jesus deserves our complete attention. To everyone who has saving faith in Jesus Christ, they have a place in heaven for eternity.

CHAPTER 3

Revelation Chapter 4

TIMELINE: The timeline jumps from John's day to a time in the future. Chapter 4 begins by saying, *"After these things,"* which suggests something happens between the end of chapter three and the beginning of chapter 4. This could be when the rapture happens. In chapter 4 Jesus changes directions and no longer talks to the church but talks about a future time of judgment on the earth. As this chapter begins John sees God getting ready to judge the earth. Jesus told the church in Philadelphia that He will make those who lie about being Jews (unsaved) face persecution but those who have saving faith in Jesus He will keep from great tribulation.

Sin and evil have gone wild on earth so God says it is time to judge the sin and reclaim His possession of the earth from Satan. From chapter 4 through chapter 19 John is shown the process of judging, claiming, and purifying earth from the curse of sin.

Revelation 4:1 (NKJV) After these things I looked, and behold, a door *standing* open in heaven. And the first voice which I heard *was* like a trumpet speaking with me, saying, "Come up here, and I will show you things which must take place after this."

As it starts off "after these things," it is referring to the previous thought. After these things were over, message to the churches, it looks like Jesus was finished with the ministry of the church on earth.

Revelation 4:2–3 (NKJV) [2] Immediately I was in the Spirit; and behold, a throne set in heaven, and *One* sat on the throne. [3] And He who sat there was like a jasper and a sardius stone in appearance; and *there was* a rainbow around the throne, in appearance like an emerald.

John finds himself in his spirit (his physical body couldn't enter heaven because of its sinful nature) taken to heaven and he saw God shining in His glory with the most beautiful sign of promise the rainbow above His head.

Revelation 4:4 (NKJV) [4] Around the throne *were* twenty-four thrones, and on the thrones I saw twenty-four elders sitting, clothed in white robes; and they had crowns of gold on their heads.

Who did John see with God in heaven? While there are several thoughts about it, it appears to be the raptured church. The first thing John sees as the scene changed from the things present to the things in the future is God on His throne. Then he sees church leaders on individual thrones dressed in white robes with crowns on their heads. John could be seeing the rewards ceremony. The church is receiving rewards.

Revelation 4:5–8 (NKJV) [5] And from the throne proceeded lightnings, thunderings, and voices. Seven lamps of fire *were* burning before the throne, which are the seven Spirits of God.

John sees judgments coming out from the throne. The seven spirits are the perfect Spirit of God, the Holy Spirit, who will be assisting Jesus in the coming judgment.

[6] Before the throne *there was* a sea of glass, like crystal. And in the midst of the throne, and around the throne, *were* four living creatures full of eyes in front and in back. [7] The first living creature *was* like a lion, the second living creature like a calf, the third living creature had a face like a man, and the fourth living creature *was* like a flying eagle. [8] *The* four living creatures, each having six wings, were full of eyes around and within. And they do not rest day or night, saying: "Holy, holy, holy, Lord God Almighty, Who was and is and is to come!"

Who were these four living creatures? They are angels used for specific judgments.

[9] Whenever the living creatures give glory and honor and thanks to Him who sits on the throne, who lives forever and ever, [10] the twenty-four elders fall

down before Him who sits on the throne and worship Him who lives forever and ever, and cast their crowns before the throne, saying: ¹¹ "You are worthy, O Lord, To receive glory and honor and power; For You created all things,
 And by Your will they exist[h] and were created."

Who are the twenty-four elders? Some speculate angels, others the lineage of Abraham, as well as other thoughts about who they are. They appear however to be humans who have overcome by saving faith because they have crowns and robes promised to those who overcome. The church fits this description. Everyone in heaven is worshiping God. The church lays down crowns, received as rewards for deeds of service to Christ, before God's throne.

SUMMARY. John sees spirits, which are the Holy Spirit of God, and four created creatures, which will be angels that will carry out judgments on the earth. He sees angels and the church all worshiping God, which is the key here. Judgment is coming, but God is holy and worthy of our worship. Judgment of sin is just and necessary because Holy God must judge sin. The church is placing their crowns around God's throne in adoration and praise for who He is and what He has done.

CHAPTER 4

Revelation Chapter 5

TIMELINE: In the future probably after the rapture but before the Tribulation begins.

¹ And I saw in the right *hand* of Him who sat on the throne a scroll written inside and on the back, sealed with seven seals. ² Then I saw a strong angel proclaiming with a loud voice, "Who is worthy to open the scroll and to lose its seals?" ³ And no one in heaven or on the earth or under the earth was able to open the scroll, or to look at it.

God is sitting on His throne and has in His hand an official document that is written on both sides. It has official seals, which means it is a legal and authentic documents. It has been sealed with seven drops of wax or seals with the insignia of the one who wrote it, God, which authenticates that it is His writing.

What is the document? It appears to represent a legal title deed to the earth. God who created the earth owns it but does not have possession of it. Satan has possession of the earth somewhat like a renter has possession of a house, but the landlord is the owner. As it is with the rent situation where the landlord sets certain rules for possession of his house and if the tenant violates those rules, the landlord can call for an eviction of the property. After years of misuse and overt breaking of the rules the Landlord is calling for an eviction of earth. So they look over heaven to find someone who has the ability to evict Satan from the earth and take possession of it. But they can't find anyone who is able to carry out the eviction.

⁴ So I wept much, because no one was found worthy to open and read

the scroll, or to look at it. ⁵ But one of the elders said to me, "Do not weep. Behold, the Lion of the tribe of Judah, the Root of David, has prevailed to open the scroll and to loose[] its seven seals."

John sees that no one can be found who is able to take the earth from Satan. Then one of the leaders of the church sitting on a throne near God told John not to be afraid because the promised one from Israel has endured and is capable of reclaiming earth.

⁶ And I looked, and behold, in the midst of the throne and of the four living creatures, and in the midst of the elders, stood a Lamb as though it had been slain, having seven horns and seven eyes, which are the seven Spirits of God sent out into all the earth. ⁷ Then He came and took the scroll out of the right hand of Him who sat on the throne.

Sure enough John looked and standing between God, the angels, and the raptured church was Jesus Christ. He had the appearance of having been crucified yet His appearance was different. John sees Jesus as the Lamb with seven eyes, which means that He has perfect vision over the earth and seven horns, which indicates that the Lamb had perfect power and authority to carry out righteous judgment on the earth. Then John sees Jesus move toward His Father and take the document from His hand meaning He is officially beginning the eviction process.

⁸ Now when He had taken the scroll, the four living creatures and the twenty-four elders fell down before the Lamb, each having a harp, and golden bowls full of incense, which are the prayers of the saints. ⁹ And they sang a new song, saying: "You are worthy to take the scroll, And to open its seals; For You were slain, And have redeemed us to God by Your blood Out of every tribe and tongue and people and nation, ¹⁰ And have made us kings and priests to our God; And we shall reign on the earth."

As soon as Jesus had taken the deed from God's hand, the angels and the church begin to worship with harps and have bowls full of the prayers from the saved of all ages. These prayers will be added to the prayers of those who believe during the tribulation period in chapter 8. They are prayers for justice for the sin and evil on the earth. Now Jesus is about to unleash justice so they worship and sing a new song. Divine justice is about to be served.

¹¹ Then I looked, and I heard the voice of many angels around the throne,

the living creatures, and the elders; and the number of them was ten thousand times ten thousand, and thousands of thousands, [12] saying with aloud voice: "Worthy is the Lamb who was slain To receive power and riches and wisdom, And strength and honor and glory and blessing!" [13] And every creature which is in heaven and on the earth and under the earth and such as are in the sea, and all that are in them, I heard saying: "Blessing and honor and glory and power *Be* to Him who sits on the throne, And to the Lamb, forever and ever!" [14] Then the four living creatures said, "Amen!" And the twenty-four elders fell down and worshiped Him who lives forever and ever.

John heard the sound of many voices around the throne. It was the voices of angels and the church. The Bible says there were more present than possibly could be counted and they were all together making sounds of worship. Then everyone from all over, under, and on the earth together spoke words of worship to God and His Son. The angels prepared for judgment responds and says so be it. And the church all fell down and worshiped Jesus.

SUMMARY. God holds ownership of Earth because He created it. Holy God must judge earth because of its sin. After a search for someone who would be able to take possession of the Earth and carry out judgment it was established that Jesus is the only one capable to carry out this mission. Then there is a picture in heaven of the raptured church and angels worshiping God because sin is about to be judged.

CHAPTER 5

Revelation Chapter 6

TIMELINE: Events in chapter 6 begin to happen before the tribulation as the Antichrist is revealed and the war of Ezekiel 38 and 39 is fought. Then the scene moves into the seven years of tribulation. Jesus has taken the deed out of His Father's hand to earth and is starting the eviction and judgment process. Remember the deed had seven waxy seals across the opening where it is rolled up. Under each seal are events of executing judgments during the end time. Then the time moves to the very beginning of the seven years of tribulation.

Revelation 6 (NKJV) [1] Now I saw when the Lamb opened one of the seals; and I heard one of the four living creatures saying with a voice like thunder, "Come and see." [2] And I looked, and behold, a white horse. He who sat on it had a bow; and a crown was given to him, and he went out conquering and to conquer.

John saw Jesus open the first of the wax seals. Then he heard one of the angels saying to him with an authoritative voice to come and see what's under this first seal. So John looked and he saw a white horse with someone sitting on it that held a bow. The rider received a crown and then he was on a course to conquer the world.

Who is this rider? We are not told. Some suggest this is Christ Himself and while he has many characteristic of the Savior it seems out of place that Christ is let out from behind the seal and starting the judgment, especially when Christ is the one lifting the seal.

It seems more likely this is the appearance of the Antichrist riding a white horse in appearance like Christ. He goes to earth for the purpose of conquering the earth. The Antichrist has a crown representing his coming to power over nations. The Antichrist rises in political power so this would place the opening of the first seal happening just before the first war of Gog and Magog, because the signing of the peace treaty will happen at the end of this war. This will catapult the Antichrist into world power. The signing of this treaty begins the seven years of tribulation.

³ When He opened the second seal, I heard the second living creature saying, "Come and see." ⁴ Another horse, fiery red, went out. And it was granted to the one who sat on it to take peace from the earth, and that *people* should kill one another; and there was given to him a great sword.

Then Jesus opened the second wax seal on the deed. Immediately John heard the second angel, which was set aside for carrying out judgment, telling John to come and see what's under this seal. John saw another horse but this time the horse was red. The rider will take away the peace from the earth. This is very likely the time that the first war of Gog and Magog war will take place. Perhaps it happens just after the rapture of the church but before the beginning of seven years of tribulation.

⁵ When He opened the third seal, I heard the third living creature say, "Come and see." So I looked, and behold, a black horse, and he who sat on it had a pair of scales in his hand. ⁶ And I heard a voice in the midst of the four living creatures saying, "A quart of wheat for a denarius, and three quarts of barley for a denarius; and do not harm the oil and the wine."

Then Jesus opened the third seal and another of the four angels set aside for judgment told John to come and see what was under the seal. John saw a black horse, and the rider was carrying a pair of scales in his hand. John sees food being weighed out for money. This shows food rationing because of great shortages. It will cost a full days wage for the average person to buy enough food to get by on. What was considered luxury food for people in John's day will be plentiful to the rich so they will fare very well while the working people will just barely get by.

This food rationing takes place just after the war of Ezekiel 38 and 39 is over. The Antichrist steps up and leads the world governments in signing a peace treaty. After the peace treaty is signed the seven years of tribulation begins. As a result of war and God's judgment, it is necessary to ration food because of a world shortage. So the Antichrist demands rationing by making it mandatory for everyone to take his mark, 666, on either their forehead or their wrist in order to make any purchase. This rationing and political leadership of the Antichrist opens up a worldwide alliance and political system — the rebirth of the Old Roman Empire.

[7] When He opened the fourth seal, I heard the voice of the fourth living creature saying, "Come and see." [8] So I looked, and behold, a pale horse. And the name of him who sat on it was Death, and Hades followed with him. And power was given to them over a fourth of the earth, to kill with sword, with hunger, with death, and by the beasts of the earth.

Then Jesus opens the fourth seal on the deed. John heard the voice of the fourth angel tell him to come and look at what is under this fourth seal. This time John sees a pale horse and the rider's name was Death and Hades. This is probably following the Gog and Magog war at the beginning of the seven years of tribulation. There will be a huge number killed, 1/4 of the world's population, as a result of war, famine, wild animals, and persecution of believers.

[9] When He opened the fifth seal, I saw under the altar the souls of those who had been slain for the word of God and for the testimony which they held. [10] And they cried with a loud voice, saying, "How long, O Lord, holy and true, until You judge and avenge our blood on those who dwell on the earth?" [11] Then a white robe was given to each of them; and it was said to them that they should rest a little while longer, until both *the number of* their fellow servants and their brethren, who would be killed as they *were,* was completed.

When Jesus opened the fifth seal on the deed, John saw underneath the altar believers martyred for their faith during the first of the tribulation. They were crying out asking the Lord, "How long are you going to wait before you bring justice for the torture and killing of believers by those who are ruling the earth?" Then they were told to rest under the altar for a little longer until everyone that will be saved was saved, and all of the believers that were to be killed were killed. This is probably happening somewhere toward the middle of the tribulation period. This shows us that this Divine justice is right and just.

> ¹² I looked when He opened the sixth seal, and behold, there was a great earthquake; and the sun became black as sackcloth of hair, and the moon[] became like blood. ¹³ And the stars of heaven fell to the earth, as a fig tree drops its late figs when it is shaken by a mighty wind. ¹⁴ Then the sky receded as a scroll when it is rolled up, and every mountain and island was moved out of its place. ¹⁵ And the kings of the earth, the great men, the rich men, the commanders,[] the mighty men, every slave and every free man, hid themselves in the caves and in the rocks of the mountains, ¹⁶ and said to the mountains and rocks, "Fall on us and hide us from the face of Him who sits on the throne and from the wrath of the Lamb! ¹⁷ For the great day of His wrath has come, and who is able to stand?"

The Antichrist breaks the peace treaty that he had brokered 3 1/2 years into the tribulation period (halfway), and he sends his troops into Jerusalem. The Antichrist erects an image of himself on the altar in the rebuilt temple in Jerusalem, which desecrates the temple. Then the false prophet stops all sacrifices and Jewish traditions of worship in the newly rebuilt temple. They clear out all of the articles and furniture used in worship in the temple along with anything that suggests the God of Israel.

The false prophet begins to demand people now worship their leader — the Antichrist. In the old Roman Empire citizens were directed to worship Caesar as their god and whatever he said was law. Now whatever the Antichrist says will be law.

SUMMARY. Jesus takes the scroll from His Father's hand and starts the evacuation and judgment of earth process. The tribulation begins as the false prophet goes out to create a political and a spiritual atmosphere for the Antichrist to step in and take control over all nations. The Antichrist occupied the city of Jerusalem. When the Antichrist and the false prophet set up an image on the altar in the Holy of Holies in the temple they cause sacrifice and worship to God to cease. This desecrates the temple of God and then extreme judgment begins.

CHAPTER 6

Revelation Chapter 7

TIMELINE: Chapter 6 happens during the first half of the tribulation. At the beginning of the tribulation period 144,000 Jews are saved. Before the judgments are pronounced in the previous chapter begin an angel, which has God's authority to speak, tells the angels who are about to carry out this judgment to wait until the 144,000 Jews were sealed. This is so they can't be killed until their ministry has been completed. After the witnesses have been sealed then judgments begin in the tribulation. Then time moves to the middle of the seven years of tribulation and the desecration of the temple happens.

[7] After these things I saw four angels standing at the four corners of the earth, holding the four winds of the earth, that the wind should not blow on the earth, on the sea, or on any tree.

"After these things," refers to seeing the opening of the six seals in chapter 6. Before the judgments under the first six seals are carried out, John sees four angels covering the earth, one at the four corners of the earth. They were stopping the wind from blowing — no wind anywhere on the earth. Why hold the wind? We are not told specifically but it seems to indicate the use of the power of the wind as a judgment later when it will be released.

[2] Then I saw another angel ascending from the east, having the seal of the living God. And he cried with a loud voice to the four angels to whom it was granted to harm the earth and the sea, [3] saying, "Do not harm the earth, the sea, or the trees till we have sealed the servants of our God on their foreheads."

Then John sees another angel coming from the east and he has a seal. The seal is God's sign of protections for the 144,000 from death by the Antichrist. The angels are instructed not the bring harm to the earth and the sea until these are sealed. Nature has been locked into the curse of sin since the fall of man. Judgment on the earth will start the process of the collapse and re-birth of the earth.

Referring to the angels as 'we' seems to indicate many angels are involved in the sealing process. Considering the number of witnesses that were sealed this would make sense. Each of those sealed will receive a mark on their forehead which will be the mark of God as opposed to the mark of the beast that non-believers will receive.

This mark indicates they are the property of God. Some believe this seal is salvation like Paul talks about salvation being sealed until the day of redemption. But here the purpose is to keep any physical harm from those who have been sealed, so the effect of the seal will be visible. In Revelation 9:4 it clearly says that those who possess this mark are protected from the fallout of the fifth seal.

⁴ And I heard the number of those who were sealed. One hundred *and* forty-four thousand of all the tribes of the children of Israel *were* sealed:

John tells us that he verbally heard the number of those who were sealed. This is important because it was not just an estimate of what he saw. One hundred forty-four thousand Jews sealed. A lot of speculation is made about why this specific number is given. Many make a lot about the number twelve here but the focus should be that God seals and protects His witnesses from harm until their ministry is complete. There should be no debate about the fact that all of the 144,000 thousand are Jews. That fact is very clear.

What is the purpose of the tribulation? It will bring divine justice for the sin of man on the earth. The nature of tribulation is to bring Israel to her knees so that they, for the most part, will finally accept Jesus. When that happens God will fulfill the rest of His promises made concerning Israel. The nation has never been positioned to receive these promises because of their denial of Jesus as the promised Messiah. So God partially suspended His work with Israel until the tribulation.

Revelation 7:5–8 (NKJV) ⁵ of the tribe of Judah twelve thousand were sealed; of the tribe of Reuben twelve thousand were sealed; of the tribe of Gad twelve thousand were sealed; ⁶ of the tribe of Asher twelve thousand were sealed; of the tribe of Naphtali twelve thousand were sealed; of the tribe of Manasseh twelve thousand were sealed; ⁷ of the tribe of Simeon twelve thousand were sealed; of the tribe of Levi twelve thousand were sealed; of the tribe of Issachar twelve thousand were sealed; ⁸ of the tribe of Zebulun twelve thousand were sealed; of the tribe of Joseph twelve thousand were sealed; of the tribe of Benjamin twelve thousand were sealed.

This list is not based on the division of land as Israel came into the Promised Land. Nor is it based on physical lineage. Manasseh is not the biological child of Jacob, but is adopted. Like the list of those blessed by Moses in Deuteronomy 33, this list is based on blessings/curses. Dan is left out of this list because he is not blessed, he is cursed so they did not receive this protection. Some have suggested that Dan's idolatry is the reason for his exclusion at this point. Joseph is a substitute for Ephraim (Ezek. 37:16–19). The name Ephraim has become synonymous with sin.

God specifically will use 144,000 people whom He will divinely protect from harm, so that they can be a witness of Christ to the Jewish nation and the world. The church is gone, but that doesn't stop the spreading of the gospel.

⁹ After these things I looked, and behold, a great multitude which no one could number, of all nations, tribes, peoples, and tongues, standing before the throne and before the Lamb, clothed with white robes, with palm branches in their hands, ¹⁰ and crying out with a loud voice, saying, "Salvation *belongs* to our God who sits on the throne, and to the Lamb!"

The phrase "after these things" is used again here which indicates the end of one vision and the beginning of another. We don't know how much time has elapsed between the two visions. The length of time must not be important or it would be included. This vision starts in verse 9 and continues through chapter 15, verse 4.

John sees a huge group of people so many that they couldn't be counted. This stresses the large number of Jews and Gentiles that will be saved as a result of the testimony of the 144,000. John sees in the future, after tribulation is over, the outcome of their witness. This should encourage John as he is seeing so much judgment. The outcome of their faithful witness is the salvation of a great multitude during the tribulation. While God is specifically dealing with the Jews, they are not the only ones who will be saved. All of these saved people are worshiping God saying "Salvation belongs to our God who sits on the throne and to the Lamb." In other words, God is the giver of salvation through Jesus Christ. The palm branches are reminiscent of Jesus triumphant entrance into Jerusalem beginning the Passion Week before He was crucified. The crowds are praising God the Father and the Son because salvation has been completed in their lives.

¹¹ All the angels stood around the throne and the elders and the four living creatures, and fell on their faces before the throne and worshiped God, ¹² saying: "Amen! Blessing and glory and wisdom, Thanksgiving and honor and power and might, *Be* to our God forever and ever. Amen." Everyone in heaven is praising God for His salvation. ¹³ Then one of the elders answered, saying to me, "Who are these arrayed in white robes, and where did they come from?" One of the leaders of the church asked John who these additional people were and where did they come from?

¹⁴ And I said to him, "Sir, you know." So he said to me, "These are the ones who come out of the great tribulation, and washed their robes and made them white in the blood of the Lamb.

John explains these are believers who were killed by political powers of the Antichrist because of their faith in Christ during the tribulation. This group is not a part of the 144,000 witnesses because they are sealed from harm.

¹⁵ Therefore they are before the throne of God, and serve Him day and night in His temple. And He who sits on the throne will dwell among them.

Because of their faith in Jesus they have joined a crowd standing around the throne. They are able to stand in front of the throne only because of the Lamb and His salvation.

¹⁶ They shall neither hunger anymore nor thirst anymore; the sun shall not strike them, nor any heat; ¹⁷ for the Lamb who is in the midst of the throne will shepherd them and lead them to living fountains of waters. And God will wipe away every tear from their eyes."

Hunger and thirst can't affect these saints any longer because they are no longer bound by the physical restraints of this life. All forms of discomfort have been removed as indicated by the removal of all tears.

SUMMARY. John is given a picture of the results of the 144,000 witness's ministry. People of every nation are saved during the tribulation and they will join those of saving faith from every generation going to heaven to live for eternity with God. This is after the tribulation and the millennial kingdom are over and eternity is ushered in. Even though persecutions will make it difficult, many people will be saved during the tribulation.

John is shown that the most powerful government can't stop the word of God from being spread and souls from being saved. He sees that in heaven people's activity will be to worship and praise God because of His salvation.

CHAPTER 7

Revelation Chapter 8

TIMELINE: Chapter 8 takes place in the middle of the tribulation. The Antichrist has invaded Jerusalem and has taken the temple. He desecrates the temple by setting up an image of himself on the altar (Matt. 24:15). After the desecration, the seventh seal is opened.

Revelation 8:1 (NKJV) When He opened the seventh seal, there was silence in heaven for about half an hour.

When the first six seals were opened John either heard or saw something. When the seventh seal is opened there was silence for about half an hour. While half an hour is not a long period of time, when you stand in anticipation in absolute silence it can seem like forever. The silence in heaven seems to be the calm before the great storm that leads to the end of earth as we know it. Under the seventh seal the worst of the woes or judgments are unleashed. They will be unleashed in two sections; the trumpet judgments and then the bowl or vial judgments.

Immediately after the silence John sees the seven angels ready to carry out judgments. The trumpet judgments revealed under the seventh seal will begin to be unleashed over the next few chapters.

² And I saw the seven angels who stand before God, and to them were given seven trumpets.

A trumpet was given to each of these seven angels.

³ Then another angel, having a golden censer, came and stood at the altar. He was given much incense, that he should offer *it* with the prayers of all the saints upon the golden altar which was before the throne.

After the seven angels received their trumpets another angel appeared carrying a censer made of gold. A censer is the vessel that the High Priest would use to take burning coal from the golden altar and then he would put incense on the coals, which cause a sweet smelling smoke to fill the room. The smoke and smell of the incense represents prayers reaching up to God. This angel was given a lot of incense to offer because they represented the prayers of everyone who has had saving faith in Jesus. In chapter 8 John sees the smoke of incense described by the word ALL indicating that those were the prayers of everyone who has had saving faith being heard. This is unlike where John sees believers from the tribulation period under the throne offering prayers and wondering when judgment will start.

⁴ And the smoke of the incense, with the prayers of the saints, ascended before God from the angel's hand. ⁵ Then the angel took the censer, filled it with fire from the altar, and threw *it* to the earth. And there were noises, thunderings, lightnings, and an earthquake.

The angel throwing the censer filled with fire upon the earth represents God answering the prayers of believers to execute judgment because of their persecution and all of the evil and sin of earth. When it hit earth it made loud noises like thunder and sights of lightening appeared. Then an earthquake happened. The worst troubles the world has ever experienced is starting at the middle of the tribulation.

⁶ So the seven angels who had the seven trumpets prepared themselves to sound.

Now the seven angels will begin to sound their trumpets individually announcing different parts of judgment. The first four parts of judgment affect elements of nature. They affect only one-third of the earth, which leaves two-thirds of the earth for the rest of this final judgment. The first angel puts the trumpet to his lips and begins to announce the first part of the first section of this final judgment.

⁷ The first angel sounded: And hail and fire followed, mingled with blood, and they were thrown to the earth. And a third of the trees were burned up, and all green grass was burned up.

Notice hail and fire happens just after the sounding of the first trumpet. Ice mingled with fire falls from the sky. The ice and fire was also mingled with the blood and together it burned up one-third of the trees, but notice it burned up all of the grass. Some believe this is a description of a nuclear war. Then the second angel put the trumpet to his lips and sounded more impending judgment is on the way.

⁸ Then the second angel sounded: And *something* like a great mountain burning with fire was thrown into the sea, and a third of the sea became blood. ⁹ And a third of the living creatures in the sea died, and a third of the ships were destroyed.

One-third of the salt water on earth from the seas is turned to blood just like the Nile River did during the plagues of Egypt. This causes one-third of all ships on the seas of earth to be destroyed because they can't navigate through the blood. Also one-third of earth's sea creatures was killed as a result of the blood. John describes a great mountain burning with fire being thrown into the sea which could describe a volcano.

Then angel number three sounds his trumpet.

¹⁰ Then the third angel sounded: And a great star fell from heaven, burning like a torch, and it fell on a third of the rivers and on the springs of water. ¹¹ The name of the star is Wormwood. A third of the waters became wormwood, and many men died from the water, because it was made bitter.

Then John saw a huge star burning like a torch fall and affect one-third of the rivers and springs of fresh water on the earth. Some suggest this might be a meteor but there is no reason not to believe it is literally a falling star. Now one-third of the earth's water supply, fresh and salt, has been polluted and can't be used. The name Wormwood is a curious name for the star. There is no evidence by astrologists that there was a star named Wormwood in John's day. Wormwood appears to have been a medicine used at this time in history to get rid of worms in a person's intestine. It was a very bitter tasting medicine. Wormwood as a medicine tasted bad but it didn't kill people and clearly many people will die from drinking this polluted water. So if the intention of the name is to be identified with this medicine, the effect is opposite to what the medicine was usually used for — instead of healing it killed.

Then the fourth angel sounded the judgment cry.

¹² Then the fourth angel sounded: And a third of the sun was struck, a third of the moon, and a third of the stars, so that a third of them were darkened. A third of the day did not shine, and likewise the night.

One-third of earth's sources of light were darkened.

And I looked, and I heard an angel flying through the midst of heaven, saying with a loud voice, "Woe, woe, woe to the inhabitants of the earth, because of the remaining blasts of the trumpet of the three angels who are about to sound!"

The King James and versions translated from it say that John heard an angel flying. The ESV, NIV and other versions which are translated from older manuscripts say that John heard an eagle flying. A person normally can't hear an eagle or angels fly. It seems that this is a picture of an angel flying authoritatively like an eagle. This angel shouts to the earth that great woes are coming. The word 'woe' is repeated three times to emphasize just how terrible the remaining three trumpets will be for those who inhabit the earth.

SUMMARY. This chapter begins with thirty minutes of silence and then devastating judgments begin to unfold. This judgment will lead to the end of the world as it is now. Incense is burnt in a censer which represented God receiving the prayers of all of who have been saved. Their prayers are for justice and holiness in the world is about to be answered.

Four of the seven angels have sounded their trumpets announcing judgments. These first four judgments effects the natural elements on the earth such as hail, fire and blood mingled together. This mixture of fire burns one-third of all of the trees on the earth and all of the grass. Then a huge mountain falls and pollutes one-third of all of the seas killing all life within them and destroying ships that sail on them. John then sees a huge burning star fall which pollutes one-third of the freshwater supply on the earth. John sees, after the fourth trumpet sounds, one-third of the earth's source of light darkened. With one-third of the water supply tainted and one-third of the source of natural light darkened it will stop the growth cycle of the food supply in one-third of the world.

After the sounding of these four trumpets John hears an angel flying like an eagle across the sky saying, "Woe, Woe, Woe on the inhabitants of earth." This angel was warning about the severity of the last three trumpet judgments which are the last of this first part of final judgment.

CHAPTER 8

Revelation Chapter 9

TIMELINE: Time moves to just after the midpoint of the tribulation into the first part of the second half. The second half of the tribulation is referred to as "The Great tribulation" because the woe's greatly increase in intensity.

Four of the seven angels have already sounded their horns. The angels one by one announce the next judgment in this first of a two part series of judgments found under the seventh seal. The judgments of the first four trumpets affected elements of the earth — water and vegetation. The fifth thru seventh trumpets bring demonic judgments on the earth. In spite of the fact that there is hell on earth in these judgments people still refuse to repent.

Revelation 9:1-21 (NKJV) [1] Then the fifth angel sounded: And I saw a star fallen from heaven to the earth. To him was given the key to the bottomless pit.

John saw a "fallen" star. The word "fallen" is a perfect tense participle, having previously fallen and now being in a fallen state. John did not actually see the fall, he saw what had happened many years before. John saw the fallen Satan. What about the star "wormwood" that fell to the earth in the previous chapter? Is wormwood and the star described here the same? It could be but that raises questions about the time of the falling. The effects of wormwood brought death to many people who drank the water. Satan has affected everything on earth. They are probably not the same thing. We know that Satan fell and it appears that he enticed one-third of the angels in heaven to rebel with him (Revelation 12:4 if you understand the dragon who with his tail drew 1/3 of stars from heaven and cast them to earth as

Satan's rebellion — some view this as Satan causing meteors to fall from heaven to earth during the tribulation). Satan's rebellion would have had to occur around the creation time because we see Satan in the Garden of Eden tempting Eve.

It appears that Satan will be restricted from having access to heaven forever during the second half of the tribulation period. Satan has had some kind of access to God through time. We see Him, in the book of Job, talking to God about Job. The focus of this chapter is the fact that John sees the fallen Satan who is given the key to hell during tribulation.

[2] *And he opened the bottomless pit, and smoke arose out of the pit like the smoke of a great furnace. So the sun and the air were darkened because of the smoke of the pit.*

Satan takes the key and unlocks the door of hell. This is the bottomless pit and not the lake of fire. When he does, dark smoke completely fills the sky above him. The abyss, place of death, hell, and hades are names given to the place of death for non-believers waiting for eternal judgment. The lake of fire is the eternal destination after the White Throne Judgment for non-believers. It appears that there are compartments in hell for different purposes around the lake of fire.

The abyss is where demons are locked up. Where did these locked up demons come from? Many speculate that they are the angels that failed in their mission on earth before the flood in Genesis. This is when the great flood came upon the earth. These angels, it is believed, inhabited human bodies and called *the Sons of God*. They lusted after and slept with *the daughters of men*. In the book of Jude it says that these angels *who did not keep their proper domain* were chained under the earth in the abyss. These fallen angels that God had cast into the abyss could be who Satan releases. Whoever they are, Satan will use them as an army to help him carry out evil upon the earth.

[3] *Then out of the smoke locusts came upon the earth. And to them was given power, as the scorpions of the earth have power.*

Out of the smoke came something that John describes as locusts and they fill the earth. The locusts described here were not like any locusts we know about. They are described as having power like scorpions. Locusts were used by God for judgment in the plagues on Egypt. But these tools of judgment are more fierce than any previously. These ferocious creatures appear to be the demons released to help Satan bring greater pain to the earth than he has ever done before.

⁴ They were commanded not to harm the grass of the earth, or any green thing, or any tree, but only those men who do not have the seal of God on their foreheads.

Normal locusts have a natural instinct to destroy vegetation so these are not just normal locusts. These demons were given the sting of scorpions but could not harm the trees and vegetation of the earth nor those who have been saved and were sealed by God.

⁵ And they were not given *authority* to kill them, but to torment them *for* five months. Their torment *was* like the torment of a scorpion when it strikes a man.

They could not kill or torment the saved because they were sealed, but they will torment the unrepentant sinners for five months with the sting of a scorpion. A severe sting of a scorpion is said to have these symptoms: widespread numbness, difficulty swallowing, a thick tongue, blurred vision, roving eye movements, seizures, salivation, and difficulty breathing.

⁶ In those days men will seek death and will not find it; they will desire to die, and death will flee from them.

The effects of the stings will be so severe that people will try to commit suicide, but won't be able to. These attempts for death may add to their physical pain.

⁷ The shape of the locusts was like horses prepared for battle. On their heads were crowns of something like gold, and their faces *were* like the faces of men.

John describes the appearance of locusts. They look like locusts but have tails like scorpions. He says they were shaped like very fit horses. These locusts, scorpion, horse-like beings were wearing crowns that had appearance like gold. These strange looking creatures had faces like men.

⁸ They had hair like women's hair, and their teeth were like lions' *teeth*.
⁹ And they had breastplates like breastplates of iron, and the sound of their wings *was* like the sound of chariots with many horses running into battle.

¹⁰ They had tails like scorpions, and there were stings in their tails. Their power *was* to hurt men five months.

There is a lot of speculation as to what John is really describing. Some believe they are helicopters. The men's face describes the bubble front with lights on it, and the scorpion tail describes the tail of the helicopter. The wings would be obvious, and the hair and teeth may describe articles of warfare. The argument for this interpretation is that these could be nuclear helicopters bringing this kind of pain with nuclear aftermath. Then there are those who believe these are literal locusts, with these special features described, who are demon possessed. More likely they are demons with the described characteristics to bring intense pain upon the unsaved. The prophet Joel describes locusts and lions like horses galloping to war to emphasize the severity of judgment.

The focus is NOT on what this creature is. The focus is that John saw Satan releasing some help from hell and they had the power to inflict great pain. So much pain that many will try to commit suicide. They have this great power but that power is limited by God so they can't destroy vegetation and can't kill anyone. God further limited their power so that they could not inflict pain on true believers. This will be a demonic invasion that will bring horror to the earth. This intense torment will last for five months and will take place sometime after the middle in the first part of the second half of the seven years of the tribulation

¹¹ And they had as king over them the angel of the bottomless pit, whose name in Hebrew *is* Abaddon, but in Greek he has the name Apollyon.

Then John is introduced to the king of the Abyss. His name in Hebrew is Abaddon which is often translated as destruction and is closely associated with death and the grave. In Greek the name is translated Apollyon which has a sense of personality to it. These names seems to show that this destruction is personal to both king and angel.

¹² One woe is past. Behold, still two more woes are coming after these things.

John has seen four angels pronouncing different judgments on the environment and vegetation of earth. Then John sees a woe or judgment pronounced that effects lost humans with devastating pain for five months. Now

John is being told that there are two more of these judgments coming that will affect everything.

13 Then the sixth angel sounded: And I heard a voice from the four horns of the golden altar which is before God,

Now the sixth angel steps up and sounds the trumpet call for judgment. This sixth trumpet judgment is longer than the previous ones. But there appears to be a break during this judgment from chapter 10:1 through 11:13. During this break John actually participates in the events and then goes back to being a witness of the events of final judgments.

A voice from the four horns of the golden altar appears to be someone other than God speaking. The golden altar before God gives a picture of the temple and the way it was laid out. The golden altar was placed in the Holy of Holies, the place that represented the presence of God. On this altar the incense was burnt representing prayers offered to God. This altar covered with gold had a projection, or a protruding part, on each corner. The voice appears to come from these projections on the corners of the golden altar.

14 saying to the sixth angel who had the trumpet, "Release the four angels who are bound at the great river Euphrates."

These four angels appear to be fallen angels who have been constrained from bringing Satan's pain upon the earth until the time that the sixth angel of judgment was given the authority to release them.

15 So the four angels, who had been prepared for the hour and day and month and year, were released to kill a third of mankind.

These four fallen angels were prepared for just this assignment and were released to kill one-third of the earth's population. One-third of the land and water supply have already been killed and now the inhabitants.

16 Now the number of the army of the horsemen *was* two hundred million; I heard the number of them.

This destruction will make WW2 look insignificant. Today the world's population is about 7.5 billion and growing. Remember in chapter 6, one-fourth of the world's population is killed which by current population would be 1.8 billion people killed in the judgment of Revelation six. That human loss would leave about 5.7 billion people alive. Killing 1/3 of these 5.7 billion would be around 1.88 billion people killed in the judgment described here.

That means that there was a total of somewhere around 3.68 billion people killed in these two judgments. Who are these people that have been killed? We are not told. It has been speculated that it could be people on North and South America (a population of around one billion) and other continents leaving the newly resurrected Roman Empire and Israel for the final war. We don't know where these deaths will take place.

Two hundred million is a huge number. But who is this huge army? It has been thought that this army had to be an army of China because they were the only ones big enough to have an army that size. But today India has the possibility to come close and a coalition of some of other nations could raise that size of an army. But when you look at the details of this army it does not appear to be a human army. It seems this is probably an army of demonic creatures Satan released from the abyss.

There will be an army from the east coming during the sixth bowl judgment which probably will be an army from China but the size of that army is not given.

¹⁷ And thus I saw the horses in the vision: those who sat on them had breastplates of fiery red, hyacinth blue, and sulfur yellow; and the heads of the horses *were* like the heads of lions; and out of their mouths came fire, smoke, and brimstone.

These were not ordinary horses. They breathed fire out of their mouths and their heads looked like lions but they were ridden like a horse. In the 2nd chapter of Joel it tells about horses having a sound like chariots that leap over mountain tops. Some believe that John was describing futuristic military equipment. This seems unlikely because it fits together smoothly to view these as demon-like horses ridden by demon soldiers led by four demons or fallen angels.

¹⁸ By these three *plagues* a third of mankind was killed — by the fire and the smoke and the brimstone which came out of their mouths.

Think about the some 1.88 billion people killed at this time. What a nightmare for those who are left. With that many dead bodies to dispose of just think of the stench of all the decaying bodies.

¹⁹ For their power is in their mouth and in their tails; for their tails *are* like serpents, having heads; and with them they do harm.

The tails of the horses are like serpents or snakes with heads and mouths. Just think about how lethal the power of each horse will be.

[20] But the rest of mankind, who were not killed by these plagues, did not repent of the works of their hands, that they should not worship demons, and idols of gold, silver, brass, stone, and wood, which can neither see nor hear nor walk.

The some 3.82 billion people left on earth still will not repent of their sin and continue to follow the Antichrist. They were given time to repent but they will not accept Christ's grace.

[21] And they did not repent of their murders or their sorceries or their sexual immorality or their thefts.

Murder could include those who were killed for not worshiping the Antichrist, abortion, euthanasia, and genetic engineering as well as terrorism and meanness. God will bring justice for the murders of the innocent. They didn't repent of using magic potions and drugs. Sorceries also included trying to communicate with the dead and all forms of magic. They didn't repent of their sexual looseness and perverted behaviors. Nor did they repent for stealing.

SUMMARY: John sees the fall of Satan, which happened in the past. Then John sees Satan given a key to Hades and Satan opens the abyss which unleashes a huge demonic army. These demons will have power to bring great pain to unbelievers who in their torment will try to commit suicide but will be unsuccessful.

As the sixth trumpet sounds and John hears a voice coming out of the protruding corners of the golden altar located in front of God. The voice instructs the sixth angel of judgment to unleash the four fallen angels to lead the demon army. This demon army will kill one-third of the population of earth. This demon army will be two hundred million strong riding demonic horses with tails like serpents. Despite all of the death and torment, the nations left will not repent and acknowledge Jesus Christ as Lord.

CHAPTER 9

Revelation Chapter 10

TIMELINE: This scene will happen after the Antichrist has captured and desecrated the temple at the end of the first 3 1/2 years of the tribulation. Six trumpet judgments have already sounded and this is a break before the seventh trumpet sounds.

Revelation 10:1–11 (NKJV) I saw still another mighty angel coming down from heaven, clothed with a cloud. And a rainbow *was* on his head, his face *was* like the sun, and his feet like pillars of fire.

The angel appears to be in addition to the four angels seen in chapter 9. Some older commentaries said that this angel was Jesus. There are many comparable descriptive phrases to Jesus used in chapter 1; however, this seems unlikely. This mighty angel represents the divine power of God and His Son in this judgment.

² He had a little book open in his hand. And he set his right foot on the sea and *his* left *foot* on the land, ³ and cried with a loud voice, as *when* a lion roars. When he cried out, seven thunders uttered their voices.

What is in this book? We are not told but it appears to be the worst of the judgments that are yet to come. The angel is pictured as having one foot on the sea and one foot on the land showing that God has power over all of the earth. The seven thunders speak of the power of God's judgment.

⁴ Now when the seven thunders uttered their voices, I was about to write; but I heard a voice from heaven saying to me, "Seal up the things which the seven thunders uttered, and do not write them." ⁵ The angel whom I saw standing on the sea and on the land raised up his hand to heaven ⁶ and

swore by Him who lives forever and ever, who created heaven and the things that are in it, the earth and the things that are in it, and the sea and the things that are in it, that there should be delay no longer,

The angel is pronouncing God's final set of judgments. John was about to write down what he was seeing, and he was suddenly stopped and instructed not to write down what he was now seeing. Why? Well we can only assume that these final judgments are so terrible the angel caused him to pause and prepare himself for what he was about to see.

⁷ but in the days of the sounding of the seventh angel, when he is about to sound, the mystery of God would be finished, as He declared to His servants the prophets.

When the next seven judgments are carried out that will be the end of the process of taking possession of the earth. Then the Messiah will rule on earth in peace for 1,000 years as Old Testament prophets had prophesied.

⁸ Then the voice which I heard from heaven spoke to me again and said, "Go, take the little book which is open in the hand of the angel who stands on the sea and on the earth." ⁹ So I went to the angel and said to him, "Give me the little book." And he said to me, "Take and eat it; and it will make your stomach bitter, but it will be as sweet as honey in your mouth."

John is instructed to take the book of these last judgments and thoroughly study it to have a good understanding of them. When you do, the thought of the depth of judgments coming will make you sick at your stomach. But the thought of God's divine justice being administered will be like a sweet taste in your mouth.

¹⁰ Then I took the little book out of the angel's hand and ate it, and it was as sweet as honey in my mouth. But when I had eaten it, my stomach became bitter. ¹¹ And he said to me, "You must prophesy again about many peoples, nations, tongues, and kings."

SUMMARY: John sees a break between the judgments that occurred at the middle and at the beginning of the second half of the tribulation. Now the last of series of judgments will begin.

CHAPTER 10

Revelation Chapter 11

TIMELINE: The two witnesses will appear around the beginning of the second half of the tribulation after the desecration of the temple. They will be sealed for 1260 days, which is a couple of weeks shy of 3 1/2 years, and will be removed just a few weeks before the battle of Armageddon.

John is told of three great woes and he has seen two revealed (the judgments under the seals and the six of the trumpet judgments). He awaits to see what kind of judgment will come after the seventh trumpet sounds. Chapter 11 gives an account of the measuring of the temple, of the two witnesses of God, of the sounding of the seventh trumpet, and what followed after it.

Revelation 11:1–2 (NKJV) [1] Then I was given a reed like a measuring rod. And the angel stood, saying, "Rise and measure the temple of God, the altar, and those who worship there. [2] But leave out the court which is outside the temple, and do not measure it, for it has been given to the Gentiles. And they will tread the holy city underfoot *for* forty-two months.

Reference of measuring the temple seems to go back to prophecy given in a vision to Ezekiel, found in Ezekiel 40.

Ezekiel 40:3–5 (NKJV) [3] He took me there, and behold, *there was* a man whose appearance *was* like the appearance of bronze. He had a line of flax and a measuring rod in his hand, and he stood in the gateway. [4] And the man said to me, "Son of man, look with your eyes and hear with your ears, and fix your mind on everything I show you; for you *were* brought here so that I might show *them* to you. Declare to the house of Israel everything you see." [5] Now there was a wall all around the outside of the temple. In the man's hand was a measuring rod six cubits *long, each being a* cubit and a handbreadth; and he measured the width of the wall structure, one rod; and the height, one rod.

The explanation of either is not so clear. It seems likely that the vision in Ezekiel compared the size of Solomon's temple and not to the rebuilding of Zerubbabel's temple or the renovation of Herod because they were not exactly the same. Perhaps the most likely explanation is that John is told to measure the original temple of Solomon to shew the exactness to the one to be rebuilt in Jerusalem before the middle of the tribulation.

Revelation 11:3–19 (NKJV) [3] And I will give *power* to my two witnesses, and they will prophesy one thousand two hundred and sixty days, clothed in sackcloth." [4] These are the two olive trees and the two lampstands standing before the God of the earth. [5] And if anyone wants to harm them, fire proceeds from their mouth and devours their enemies. And if anyone wants to harm them, he must be killed in this manner. [6] These have power to shut heaven, so that no rain falls in the days of their prophecy; and they have power over waters to turn them to blood, and to strike the earth with all plagues, as often as they desire.

When the desecration of the temple happens then the appearance of two witnesses will occur. This will be at the beginning of the second half of the tribulation period. They will witness for just short of three and one-half years or just before Christ returns. The focus here is that the true gospel will be preached until just before Jesus returns.

The two witnesses will be given power so that when their lives are threatened they can speak and fire comes out of their mouths and consumes the aggressor. The witnesses will not be destroyed and will have God-given power to do miraculous signs to authenticate the gospel message and many will be saved as they preach.

[7] When they finish their testimony, the beast that ascends out of the bottomless pit will make war against them, overcome them, and kill them.

Just as soon as they complete their mission, just a few days shy of three and one-half years, the seal is removed and the Antichrist overcomes the witnesses and kills them.

8 And their dead bodies *will lie* in the street of the great city which spiritually is called Sodom and Egypt, where also our Lord was crucified.

The bodies of the witnesses will be left on a street in Jerusalem. Jerusalem is called Sodom and Egypt because of their great sins and idolatry. Remember the political system of the Antichrist will move into Jerusalem at the midpoint of the seven years of tribulation. The hatred against these witnesses will be so great that the Antichrist will not allow a burial. The Antichrist wants the world to see that he has defeated these witnesses.

9 Then *those* from the peoples, tribes, tongues, and nations will see their dead bodies three-and-a-half days, and not allow their dead bodies to be put into graves.

The sight of the dead witnesses will capture worldwide attention and people from all over the earth will be able to see their corpses lying in the street of Jerusalem, probably by satellite.

10 And those who dwell on the earth will rejoice over them, make merry, and send gifts to one another, because these two prophets tormented those who dwell on the earth.

The world is jubilant at the sight of these dead witnesses! Remember these witnesses had killed anyone who tried to harm them and they had been a challenge to the Antichrist and his politics. That's why the world rejoices at their death.

11 Now after the three-and-a-half days the breath of life from God entered them, and they stood on their feet, and great fear fell on those who saw them.

After 3 1/2 days God breathes the breath of life back into them. What a sight that will be as the world sees those who were dead now alive again. The world will be terrified.

12 And they heard a loud voice from heaven saying to them, "Come up here." And they ascended to heaven in a cloud, and their enemies saw them.

Then the world heard a loud voice from heaven. Remember, the world has been watching the witnesses in the street-probably by satellite-so they will be able to hear this voice. It says to these witnesses to come on up to heaven. The world that was rejoicing suddenly saw the witnesses resurrected and they were terrified.

13 In the same hour there was a great earthquake, and a tenth of the city fell. In the earthquake seven thousand people were killed, and the rest were afraid and gave glory to the God of heaven.

The ascension into heaven by the witnesses happens just a few days before Christ appears and destroys all of the armies of earth. After the resurrection of the witnesses there will be a great earthquake and one-tenth of the city of Jerusalem will be destroyed. Jerusalem today has a total land area of 48.3 square miles. One tenth of the city would be about a 4.8 square mile area that is destroyed by an earthquake. In this earthquake 7,000 people will be killed. The population of Jerusalem in 2011 was 809,428 so if the population were to remain around this number then somewhere around 802,428 people in the city of Jerusalem will believe and give glory to God after seeing Him call these witnesses to life and into heaven. The city of Jerusalem, the center of Jewish life, will finally accept Jesus as Messiah. They rejected Jesus when He was on the earth the first time and have never, as a whole, accepted Jesus Christ as the promised Messiah until this time at the last of the seven year tribulation.

¹⁴ The second woe is past. Behold, the third woe is coming quickly.

John is about to hear the sounding of the seventh and last trumpet and see the judgments they will bring. He tells us that the second woe is past. The first woe was the judgment found under the seals of the scroll. Then in chapter 8 under the seventh seal the seven trumpet judgment were announced which was the second woe. Now the third and final woe is announced at the sounding of the seventh trumpet these judgments, known as the bowl or vial judgments, will take place during the last few days of life as we know it.

¹⁵ Then the seventh angel sounded: And there were loud voices in heaven, saying, "The kingdoms of this world have become *the kingdoms* of our Lord and of His Christ, and He shall reign forever and ever!"

WOW, what a wonderful announcement! John heard loud voices in heaven announcing that the earth is becoming the Kingdom of Jesus Christ. This is His coming millennial kingdom.

¹⁶ And the twenty-four elders who sat before God on their thrones fell on their faces and worshiped God, ¹⁷ saying: "We give You thanks, O Lord God Almighty, The One who is and who was and who is to come, Because You have taken Your great power and reigned. ¹⁸ The nations were angry, and

Your wrath has come, And the time of the dead, that they should be judged, And that You should reward Your servants the prophets and the saints, And those who fear Your name, small and great, And should destroy those who destroy the earth."

John saw the elders, probably leaders of the church, who were seated around the throne of God, fall on their faces to worship God because Christ has taken possession of earth. After taking possession of the earth will come judgment for all the dead and reward for the faithful believers of Christ during the tribulation.

¹⁹ Then the temple of God was opened in heaven, and the ark of His covenant was seen in His temple. And there were lightnings, noises, thunderings, an earthquake, and great hail.

The opening of the temple is the perfect temple in heaven. The ark indicates God's perfect presence. Those present are offering perfect worship and praise to God. The Antichrist stopped all worship in the temple and directed worship to himself. The perfect temple in heaven probably is opened after the desecration of the temple in Jerusalem.

Then John sees some awful things happening — lightning and thunder, great noise, an earthquake, and great hail. There is a picture of Holy God, executing wrath and judgment which is perfectly justified because sin had corrupted the earth and the temple. This will be an answer to the prayers for justice of believers who had been tortured and martyred for their faith.

SUMMARY: John is assured that God's exact standards will endure until the very end by the measuring of the temple. John sees that even though the witness of the church is gone, Christ will have witnesses to His saving grace and Satan can't stop it until Christ is finished with them. Two woes have already been exposed and now John is given a glimpse into the unveiling of the third woe. John hears the announcement that the earth will become the promised kingdom of Christ on earth where He will reign over Israel and all nations from the New City of Jerusalem where Jesus is the perfect temple.

CHAPTER 11

Revelation Chapter 12

TIMELINE: Now stepping back for a moment from the later part of the seven years of the tribulation. The last of the trumpet series of judgments is revealed. John was looking into heaven at the temple of God.

Revelation 12:1–12 (NKJV) ¹ Now a great sign appeared in heaven: a woman clothed with the sun, with the moon under her feet, and on her head a garland of twelve stars. ² Then being with child, she cried out in labor and in pain to give birth.

John sees a great sign appear in heaven. Heaven here seems to be the atmosphere above the earth because John will see the sun, moon, and stars, then he will see darkness and light all at the same time.

The woman in verse 1 dominates the sky. Looking at her John sees both day and night, because the sun, moon and stars are all visible at once. The pure woman in the Old Testament refers to a faithful Israel. In the New Testament, it refers to the faithful church. Here in context it seems that the woman would be Israel because Jesus Christ was born a descendant of Israel through Mary. The woman is seen with the glory of the sun and moon reflecting the glory of the Messiah coming into the world.

The garland of twelve stars some suggest represent the twelve apostles. As a star was used in chapters 2 and 3 to represent pastors of the seven churches, the stars appear to be the apostles who were commissioned by Jesus to faithfully carry the gospel message to the world. It seems then that the focus is on the glory of God, through Jesus Christ. Jesus came to earth through the nation of Israel and His message of hope and life has been faithfully proclaimed ever since.

> ³ And another sign appeared in heaven: behold, a great, fiery red dragon having seven heads and ten horns, and seven diadems on his heads.

The red dragon represents Satan, as he is identified in verse 9. The seven heads, ten horns, and seven crowns on his head represent the government used by Satan to try and destroy Israel and stop the worship of the Child that came from her.

> ⁴ His tail drew a third of the stars of heaven and threw them to the earth. And the dragon stood before the woman who was ready to give birth, to devour her Child as soon as it was born.

Satan, Lucifer as he was known in heaven, rebelled against the authority of God. Many believe this is a reference to that rebellion where Satan led one-third all of the angels of heaven to rebel with him. They were cast out of heaven and arrived on earth. Satan and his demons were ready to destroy Jesus Christ and actively try to stop His ministry on earth.

> ⁵ She bore a male Child who was to rule all nations with a rod of iron. And her Child was caught up to God and His throne.

Here is a picture of Jesus born in Israel. It gives a prophecy of Jesus Christ ruling the earth with a just and holy form of government. Before that time is to come to pass, Jesus was crucified, which was necessary to secure salvation for mankind. He was buried but rose to life again on the third day proving His power over death. Then after forty days Jesus ascended from earth to heaven where today He sits at the right hand of the throne of God and acts as an advocate for believers before His Father.

> ⁶ Then the woman fled into the wilderness, where she has a place prepared by God, that they should feed her there one thousand two hundred and sixty days.

We have identified this woman as the nation of Israel. Here she is pictured during the last half of the tribulation. These are the Jews that will be saved during the tribulation. She is being protected from the wrath of the Antichrist. We know that many Jews will be saved and martyred during the tribulation. God will protect the nation of Israel until the end because it is a promise of God to the nation. Remember the purpose of the tribulation seems to be to bring Divine justice and to bring the nation of Israel to its knees so that she will finally accept Jesus as the Messiah. Then Israel will finally be able to receive the unfulfilled promises made by God to the nation.

⁷ And war broke out in heaven: Michael and his angels fought with the dragon; and the dragon and his angels fought, ⁸ but they did not prevail, nor was a place found for them in heaven any longer. ⁹ So the great dragon was cast out, that serpent of old, called the Devil and Satan, who deceives the whole world; he was cast to the earth, and his angels were cast out with him.

John sees Satan and some of his demons being thrown out of heaven. We were given a picture into the past to a time when Lucifer and one-third of all angels were thrown out of heaven because of their rebellion. In chapter 9 they are cast to the earth where Satan took possession. Here in verse 4 it describes that same time as well. In verse 7 Satan and his demons fought against the angel Michael and Satan was driven from heaven.

Many believe this war happened when Jesus rose from the dead they say this is described in verse 10. Others believe this describes a literal war in heaven and access to heaven was banned throughout the rest of the tribulation. That makes sense since verse 10 describes the kingdom of God and Satan being cast down.

There will be many battles in this war but at the conclusion of the Great tribulation Jesus Christ will subdue Satan. He will be cast with his demons into the bottomless pit, but not yet into the lake of fire. The Antichrist and the False Prophet will be cast in the lake of fire. Satan is not finished yet so he will not be cast into the lake of fire until after the millennial reign of Christ. After the millennial reign of Christ, Satan will be loosed from his chains. He will gather an army and will engage war against Christ. Satan and his army will be quickly defeated forever, and they will be cast into the lake of fire.

¹⁰ Then I heard a loud voice saying in heaven, "Now salvation, and strength, and the kingdom of our God, and the power of His Christ have come, for the accuser of our brethren, who accused them before our God day and night, has been cast down. ¹¹ And they overcame him by the blood of the Lamb and by the word of their testimony, and they did not love their lives to the death. ¹² Therefore rejoice, O heavens, and you who dwell in them! Woe to the inhabitants of the earth and the sea! For the devil has come down to you, having great wrath, because he knows that he has a short time."

Rejoicing is because of the power of God over Satan. It was accomplished through the blood of Jesus which gave salvation to the saints. Remember after Satan was cast to the earth and tempted Eve, she and Adam ate in disobedience to God. Then a curse for sin was pronounced. In the curse is found a prophecy about the overcoming of sin. In the 3rd chapter of Genesis, Satan is cursed and then God gives this prophecy.

Genesis 3:15 (NKJV) [15] And I will put enmity Between you and the woman, And between your seed and her Seed; He shall bruise your head, And you shall bruise His heel."

There will be conflict between Satan and Jesus Christ. The prophecy in this curse said one day Jesus will be killed and placed in the grave which bruised the heel of Christ because it was not a fatal blow — he rose back to life. Then the day is coming when Satan will receive a fatal blow to his head. It is fatal because he will be permanently confined to the lake of fire. So, Satan is going to cause havoc to the nation of Israel and to the church, as much as he can, to stop the growth of Christ's coming kingdom until the very end.

Satan has been permanently thrown out of heaven and is very busy causing all the destruction he can because he knows the end is coming soon. All of heaven is rejoicing at the approaching time of Jesus taking control of the earth and judging sin.

Revelation 12:13-17 Now when the dragon saw that he had been cast to the earth, he persecuted the woman who gave birth to the male *Child*.

Satan has always actively persecuted the nation of Israel but will intensify his persecution during these last days.

[14] But the woman was given two wings of a great eagle, that she might fly into the wilderness to her place, where she is nourished for a time and times and half a time, from the presence of the serpent.

This woman with wings is Israel. She has wings to show they are carried fast to a place of protection prepared especially for her during the last 3 1/2 years. This protection is described in **Isaiah 40:31 (NKJV)** But those who wait on the Lord shall renew their strength; They shall mount up with wings like eagles, They shall run and not be weary, They shall walk and not faint. Satan has been frustrated at every turn and now he is defeated. He was first driven from heaven. Then he failed to destroy the woman's child, Christ. Then when he tried to destroy the woman herself, Israel, he fails again.

¹⁵ So the serpent spewed water out of his mouth like a flood after the woman, that he might cause her to be carried away by the flood.

This flood is Satan's response to refuge being provided for the nation of Israel. He tried to flood the places of refuge.

¹⁶ But the earth helped the woman, and the earth opened its mouth and swallowed up the flood which the dragon had spewed out of his mouth.

Jesus caused the earth to open up and swallow the water so that Israel is still safe as a place of refuge.

¹⁷ And the dragon was enraged with the woman, and he went to make war with the rest of her offspring, who keep the commandments of God and have the testimony of Jesus Christ.

This enraged Satan. So, he waged a great war with the remainder of the nation who were believers.

SUMMARY: John is reminded that the message of the gospel will be maintained throughout time. John is seeing the unfolding of the completion and fulfillment of this message. Satan rebelled against God's authority and took one-third of the angels with him out of heaven. He then waged war against Israel and God's Son who was born through the nation of Israel. Satan will continually seek to destroy the nation of Israel and Christ's church until the very end.

CHAPTER 12

Revelation Chapter 13

TIMELINE: John gets a glimpse back to the beginning of the tribulation to the rise of the Antichrist into worldwide power. He sees the false prophet who directs people's worship to the Antichrist, and Satan, the false spirit who empowers them. Then in verse 6 the scene moves to the middle of the tribulation as the Antichrist moves into Jerusalem. Then the scene changes to the last of the tribulation when the Antichrist is killed by the sword of Christ, God's Word.

Revelation 13:1–18 (NKJV) [1] Then I stood on the sand of the sea. And I saw a beast rising up out of the sea, having seven heads and ten horns, and on his horns ten crowns, and on his heads a blasphemous name. [2] Now the beast, which I saw was like a leopard, his feet were like *the feet of* a bear, and his mouth like the mouth of a lion. The dragon gave him his power, his throne, and great authority. [3] And *I saw* one of his heads as if it had been mortally wounded, and his deadly wound was healed. And all the world marveled and followed the beast.

Notice the similarity of the beast rising up out of the sea and the dragon in chapter 12. Here the beast (Antichrist) from the sea is seen as having seven heads and ten horns with a blasphemous name written on the heads, which is possibly the name of Satan. There are seven heads, which are kings, and ten horns and crowns on the beast head. The revived Roman Empire will be made up of ten strong nations (the ten horns of power over these nations, and crowns a sign of his authority over them) and seven heads. We are told that three of these ten nations will try to leave this coalition and their kings will be removed. There is a family resemblance of this beast and the Dragon (Satan). It is suggested that the Dragon is calling the beast out of the sea (out of the political world where he was) and giving him power and authority. This moves time back to the beginning of the tribulation.

John saw the beast with a severe wound that should be fatal but he saw the wound healed. Satan does not have power over life and death. Verse 3 says *as if* it had been killed and appears to come back to life. The world sees this and marvels at the Antichrist's power over death. Many sees this as a picture of the Roman Empire which appeared to be dead but the Antichrist brought it back to life and people marveled at his abilities.

⁴ So they worshiped the dragon who gave authority to the beast; and they worshiped the beast, saying, "Who *is* like the beast? Who is able to make war with him?" ⁵ And he was given a mouth speaking great and blasphemies, and he was given authority to continue for forty-two months.

The world worships the dragon (Satan) whom they believed gave the Antichrist power to resurrect this great empire. They also worshiped the beast (the Antichrist) saying that he has the power and the ability to defeat any enemy. Remember he is credited for bringing peace to Israel by signing a worldwide peace treaty. The beast spoke with great authority and blasphemed against God. He breaks the seven year peace treaty after only three and one-half years. This is a glimpse back to the beginning of the seven years of tribulation as the Antichrist comes to power and it goes until the middle of the tribulation as he desecrates the temple. Then he has power and authority to bring great pain for three and one-half years.

⁶ Then he opened his mouth in blasphemy against God, to blaspheme His name, His tabernacle, and those who dwell in heaven. ⁷ It was granted to him to make war with the saints and to overcome them. And authority was given him over every tribe, tongue, and nation.

The Antichrist, under the authority of Satan, has overcome many believers. The Antichrist cursed God and moved into Jerusalem, took over the temple and put an image of himself on the altar. Then the False Prophet directed worship to the Antichrist. He controls every nation left in the world.

⁸ All who dwell on the earth will worship him, whose names have not been written in the Book of Life of the Lamb slain from the foundation of the

world. ⁹ If anyone has an ear, let him hear. ¹⁰ He who leads into captivity shall go into captivity; he who kills with the sword must be killed with the sword. Here is the patience and the faith of the saints.

Every unsaved person on earth worships the Antichrist. Then a warning is given that everyone needs to listen to. The Antichrist, who leads true believers into captivity on earth, will himself be brought into the captivity after the tribulation is over. He will physically die by the sword of Christ, God's Word, at the end of the tribulation. Then he is thrown into the lake of fire. With this knowledge believers can find strength in their time of danger.

Then John sees another beast that looks like a lamb with two horns, but sounds like a dragon.

¹¹ Then I saw another beast coming up out of the earth, and he had two horns like a lamb and spoke like a dragon.

This beast that John sees has a peaceful appearance but sounds like a beast. He is coming from the earth rather than the sea.

¹² And he exercises all the authority of the first beast in his presence, and causes the earth and those who dwell in it to worship the first beast, whose deadly wound was healed.

This beast (the false prophet) is not in competition with the beast from the sea (Antichrist) but rather supports all that he does. Notice it says "in his presence" which seems to indicate the Antichrist controls what he does. Satan gives the False Prophet power to do what appears to be miracles and at the middle of the tribulation when the Antichrist moves into the temple, the False Prophet will lead people to worship the beast from the sea who appeared to have power over death.

¹³ He performs great signs, so that he even makes fire come down from heaven on the earth in the sight of men. ¹⁴ And he deceives those who dwell on the earth by those signs which he was granted to do in the sight of the beast, telling those who dwell on the earth to make an image to the beast who was wounded by the sword and lived.

God allowed Satan to give the false prophet power to do many things that appear to be miracles by which he deceives people. He has made a statue of the Antichrist at the middle of the tribulation and leads people to worship it.

¹⁵ He was granted *power* to give breath to the image of the beast, that

the image of the beast should both speak and cause as many as would not worship the image of the beast to be killed.

God allows Satan to give power to the false prophet to cause this statue in the temple to appear to breathe and speak like a person. He will have killed anyone who will not worship. This begins at the middle of the tribulation and is part of the desecration of the temple.

[16] He causes all, both small and great, rich and poor, free and slave, to receive a mark on their right hand or on their foreheads, [17] and that no one may buy or sell except one who has the mark or the name of the beast, or the number of his name. [18] Here is wisdom. Let him who has understanding calculate the number of the beast, for it is the number of a man: His number is 666.

Then the false prophet causes everyone to receive a mark on their right hand or on their forehead in order to transact any business at all. This happens during the first half of the tribulation as the Antichrist puts into place a rationing system of food and other things necessary for life because there will be great shortages. What is the mark? It is identified as the number of the Antichrist — 666. This number is to characterize and not to identify the Antichrist. Six is the number of man. He is characterized as having the number of man and not a god. This man is part of a trinity of men and not gods.

Notice the similarity of the beast from the sea to the emperor Nero who John would have been familiar with. According to several of the secular historians who wrote during the time of John, Nero was responsible for many atrocities against Christians like dipping them into oil and then setting them on fire to be used as lights in his garden. John, who tradition says was dipped in hot oil but did not die from it was banished to Patmos.

John, when he saw this picture, could identify with the persecution of believers by this future political ruler who wanted to be worshiped as a god and the cruel forms of torment for those who would not worship him. While some say this is a picture of Nero and was fulfilled many years ago, it seems clear by way of the context that this is a picture of a future leader during the end of days. The point is the beast from the sea is evil and should be avoided. He is destined to failure upon failure as seen in the next few chapters.

SUMMARY: The second and third parts of the false trinity are introduced in this chapter. The beast from the sea, the Antichrist, and the beast from the earth — the False Prophet, are shown to be empowered by Satan and perform what appears to be miracles. This entices people to worship the Antichrist. The false prophet will direct worship to a statue of the Antichrist erected in the temple in Jerusalem. It will appear to breathe and speak and have the power to have anyone killed who will not worship the Antichrist. Everyone will have to take the name or number of the Antichrist which is 666. in order to transact any business The focus should be not so much about the number of the beast as much as on the fact that life is going to be extremely difficult for anyone who truly believes in Christ. But as mentioned in verse 10 there is strength and patience to be found as it is needed for the believer.

CHAPTER 13

Revelation Chapter 14

TIMELINE: John sees a glimpse of the destiny of the 144,000 witnesses in God's triumph over evil at the end of the tribulation. Then in the last half of the tribulation warning is given to repent. Time then moves to the end of time when Jesus destroys evil and takes possession of earth.

Revelation 14:1–20 (NKJV) ¹ Then I looked, and behold, a Lamb standing on Mount Zion, and with Him one hundred *and* forty-four thousand, having His Father's name written on their foreheads.

This must be the most beautiful picture in the world. Jesus standing on Mount Zion, the city of Jerusalem, surrounded by the 144,000 witnesses who have been given God's name on their forehead in contrast to the Antichrist number on the foreheads of non-believers. The two beast from the previous chapter are nowhere to be seen. John is given a glimpse of how it turns out in the end. Mount Zion here is a place of victory and rest for the 144,000 witnesses.

² And I heard a voice from heaven, like the voice of many waters, and like the voice of loud thunder. And I heard the sound of harpists playing their harps. ³ They sang as it were a new song before the throne, before the four living creatures, and the elders; and no one could learn that song except the hundred *and* forty-four thousand who were redeemed from the earth.

The voice of many waters pictures a powerful but peaceful sound coupled with bold loud thunder the sound of authority. John hears a song that the 144,000 witnesses alone were able to sing accompanied by harpists.

⁴ These are the ones who were not defiled with women, for they are

virgins. These are the ones who follow the Lamb wherever He goes. These were redeemed from *among* men, *being* firstfruits to God and to the Lamb. ⁵ And in their mouth was found no deceit, for they are without fault before the throne of God.

These witness' actions were righteous as true believers of the Lamb. Their ministry will be to be witnesses for Christ. They never marry or have relations with women because it would divide their time from their ministry. These were men set aside on earth and referred to as "first-fruit". In the Old Testament the first-fruit was the first fruit to appear before the harvest was ready. This first-fruit was a sign that the harvest was coming. In the New Testament it was used as a metaphor for something given in advance. In particular the Holy Spirit is given to each believer as a sign that the harvest is coming. These 144,000 are signs that the judgment is coming. In the last chapter, the two beasts were shown causing wrath upon the earth and here is God's judgment upon them for what they have done to true believers.

⁶ Then I saw another angel flying in the midst of heaven, having the everlasting gospel to preach to those who dwell on the earth — to every nation, tribe, tongue, and people — ⁷ saying with a loud voice, "Fear God and give glory to Him, for the hour of His judgment has come; and worship Him who made heaven and earth, the sea and springs of water."

John sees another angel who begins to give an invitation and warning to the inhabitants on earth. An invitation to repent and believe in Christ and a warning that Christ is about to come and will bring judgment for the sin of the world.

⁸ And another angel followed, saying, "Babylon is fallen, is fallen, that great city, because she has made all nations drink of the wine of the wrath of her fornication."

Then John sees an additional angel who is speaking to the same crowd. He talks specifically about the government of the Antichrist, called Babylon. This evil government has led the world into great sin, immorality, and blasphemy against God.

⁹ Then a third angel followed them, saying with a loud voice, "If anyone worships the beast and his image, and receives *his* mark on his forehead or on his hand, ¹⁰ he himself shall also drink of the wine of the wrath of God,

which is poured out full strength into the cup of His indignation. Thy will be tormented with fire and brimstone in the presence of Jesus and His angels.

Then John sees a third angel saying with a loud voice that if anyone takes the number of the Antichrist they will receive the wrath of God. He will be tormented with fire and brimstone in the presence of Jesus and the angels.

¹¹ And the smoke of their torment ascends forever and ever; and they have no rest day or night, who worship the beast and his image, and whoever receives the mark of his name."

The lake of fire is the destiny of everyone who rejects Jesus Christ. It is also a celebration of Jesus' victory and His judgment falling upon the beast and his followers. The smoke from this defeated Babylon goes up forever, in other words, it has been destroyed never to be revived. This is a momentary preview of hell and the lake of fire.

¹² Here is the patience of the saints; here *are* those who keep the commandments of God and the faith of Jesus.

The patience of the saints (people who are saved), refers to the long-awaited justice for the pain and suffering of the many who were martyred because of their faith in Jesus Christ. They are patiently waiting for Jesus coming and for His judgment on the Antichrist and his government.

¹³ Then I heard a voice from heaven saying to me, "Write: 'Blessed *are* the dead who die in the Lord from now on. " "Yes," says the Spirit, "that they may rest from their labors, and their works follow them."

Because of their faith these persecuted and martyred believers will be resting from the toils and pains of life in complete peace. They will be rewarded for their works of faith.

¹⁴ Then I looked, and behold, a white cloud, and on the cloud sat *One* like the Son of Man, having on His head a golden crown, and in His hand a sharp sickle. ¹⁵ And another angel came out of the temple, crying with a loud voice to Him who sat on the cloud, "Thrust in Your sickle and reap, for the time has come for You to reap, for the harvest of the earth is ripe." ¹⁶ So He who sat on the cloud thrust in His sickle on the earth, and the earth was reaped.

John sees Jesus standing on a cloud with a sickle in his hand. The sickle is a sharp, curved blade on the end of a long handle used to harvest grain in the fields. In chapter 4 they looked all over heaven to find someone worthy to take the title deed from God the Father's hand and then take possession of the earth from Satan. Sin is ripe and now it is time for the harvest. Another angel came out of the temple loudly asking Jesus to thrust the sickle upon the earth because the earth was ripe with sin and it was time to take possession.

[17] Then another angel came out of the temple which is in heaven, he also having a sharp sickle. [18] And another angel came out from the altar, who had power over fire, and he cried with a loud cry to him who had the sharp sickle, saying, "Thrust in your sharp sickle and gather the clusters of the vine of the earth, for her grapes are fully ripe."

John sees two more angels. One came from the temple in heaven with a sickle and then another angel from the altar. The angel from the altar tells the angel with the sickle to use it to gather a harvest of the fruits of this evil world. While this sounds like a final judgment John sees more coming.

[19] So the angel thrust his sickle into the earth and gathered the vine of the earth, and threw *it* into the great winepress of the wrath of God. [20] And the winepress was trampled outside the city, and blood came out of the winepress, up to the horses' bridles, for one thousand six hundred furlongs.

Notice the harvest in verses 14 and 15 used grain as an example of judgment. Here grapes and a winepress are used. In verses 17 and 18 the grapes are harvested, which are judgments for sin. Then the harvest was thrown into the winepress of God's wrath. This is perhaps the most gruesome picture in the book of Revelation. Why the two different illustrations? There are several thoughts about this but the one that seems to fit into the context is that this is a picture of Christ gathering the saved in a bloodless harvest. The grain, represents saved people, being separated from the chaff, representing the lost. Then judgment for the lost and their sin is pictured in the winepress as bloody and terminal.

So many people are involved in this judgment that the blood from the winepress flowed like wine pressed from grapes. There was so much blood it that it flows for 200 miles as deep as the height of a horses bridle from the ground (approximately four feet deep). Many have tried to identify where this lake of blood will be but we don't know for sure. That is not the focus. The focus here is the fact that judgment falls on all of the unsaved because of their unforgiven sins. The saved, on the other hand, will be triumphant and live in peace forever.

John, it appears, is given a preview of the final battle on earth — Armageddon, which will be described in a future chapter. In this battle no one escapes judgment — saints are already gone from earth.

SUMMARY: This chapter begins with a picture into the far future — after the tribulation — when Jesus Christ and the 144,000 witnesses are standing above the earth watching the great harvest. There is a harvest of people on the earth and the saved are separated from non-believers, like the chaff from the wheat, with the unsaved facing the judgment of the winepress.

CHAPTER 14

Revelation Chapter 15

TIMELINE: What's going on is hard to keep up with because everything is moving so fast from one scene to another. But John is able to keep the sequence and follow what he is shown. The last seven plagues of judgment are being given as they move toward the very last part of the second half of the tribulation.

Revelation 15:1–8 (NKJV) [1] Then I saw another sign in heaven, great and marvelous: seven angels having the seven last plagues, for in them the wrath of God is complete.

John says he saw another sign and calls it great and marvelous. In chapter 12, John describes the sign of the woman clothed with the sun as "great and marvelous." In verse 12:3 he calls the enormous red dragon just another sign. Here, in verse 1, he calls the seven angels with seven plagues great and marvelous showing these judgments are from God. These bowls are the third and final judgment. The terrible harvest of chapter 14 was not the end as it appeared to be. John now sees seven angels with seven last plagues which will happen fast and lead to the end which John was given a preview in chapter 14.

[2] And I saw *something* like a of glass mingled with fire, and those who have the victory over the beast, over his image and over his mark *and* over the number of his name, standing on the sea of glass, having harps of God.

John is seeing the 144,000 standing in heaven on the sea that reflects the fire and torches around it. These witnesses have just come out of the fire of persecution on earth and are now making heavenly music.

³ They sing the song of Moses, the servant of God, and the song of the Lamb, saying: "Great and marvelous *are* Your works, Lord God Almighty! Just and true *are* Your ways, O King of the saints!

The song that the 144,000 are singing is not really about Moses nor really of the Lamb, it is a song that talks about the Lord God Almighty and His great divine justice and the deliverance that He brought to Moses as he led Israel from the Egyptians, Christ as He rose from the dead, and those saved from the judgments of earth.

⁴ Who shall not fear You, O Lord, and glorify Your name? For *You* alone *are* holy. For all nations shall come and worship before You, For Your judgments have been manifested."

This song puts the severe judgments that are coming into prospective that they are divine, holy, and just judgments.

⁵ After these things I looked, and behold, the temple of the tabernacle of the testimony in heaven was opened.

John is seeing the temple opened. This is not the temple of Solomon or Herod or even the temple rebuilt before the middle of tribulation. It is compared to the tent used by Moses as a tabernacle which contained the ark of the covenant. The open temple represents the presence of God revealed.

⁶ And out of the temple came the seven angels having the seven plagues, clothed in pure bright linen, and having their chests girded with golden bands.

Now these last and most severe of the judgments begin.

⁷ Then one of the four living creatures gave to the seven angels seven golden bowls full of the wrath of God who lives forever and ever. ⁸ The temple was filled with smoke from the glory of God and from His power, and no one was able to enter the temple till the seven plagues of the seven angels were completed.

The smoke represents the glory of God that completely filled the temple. No one could enter the temple until this divine judgment of God is completed.

SUMMARY: This chapter is a pause between the trumpet judgments and the bowl judgments. The pause. This pause emphasizes the terrible nature of this judgment.. It also shows that these terrible judgments are necessary to judge the great sin of the earth.

CHAPTER 15

Revelation Chapter 16

TIMELINE: The scene has moved to the last few weeks of the second half of tribulation. After the last of the trumpet judgements come seven final judgements which are the most severe of all the judgements on the earth. These bowl judgements were introduced in chapter 15.

Revelation 16:1–21 (NKJV) [1] Then I heard a loud voice from the temple saying to the seven angels, "Go and pour out the bowls of the wrath of God on the earth."

The first three bowl judgements are similar to the first three trumpet judgements in that they affect the earth, the sea, and the fresh water. But there are some differences. First, they are greater in intensity than the trumpet counterparts. The first three trumpet judgments were limited to 1/3 of the population. These judgements will affect all of the remaining earth. In the bowl judgements humans are affected. These bowl judgements target specifically people with the mark of the beast. These judgements are called plagues and have a similarity to the plagues of Egypt before the Exodus.

[2] So the first went and poured out his bowl upon the earth, and a foul and loathsome sores came upon the men who had the mark of the beast and those who worshiped his image. [3] Then the second angel poured out his bowl on the sea, and it became blood as of a dead *man*; and every living creature in the sea died. [4] Then the third angel poured out his bowl on the rivers and springs of water, and they became blood.

This extremely painful plague of oozing, smelly sores all over the body of those who have the mark of the beast is much like the sixth plague of Egypt found in Exodus 9:8–12. Then the second angel poured out his bowl on the sea, and it became blood as of a dead *man*; and every living creature in the sea died. Then the third angel poured out his bowl on the rivers and springs of water and they became blood. This bowl judgment causes the water in the seas to become like blood, causing all life in the sea to die. The third judgment causes all of the rivers and springs to turn to blood so that there is no fresh water that is not contaminated.

⁵ And I heard the angel of the waters saying: "You are righteous, O Lord, The One who is and who was and who is to be, Because You have judged these things. ⁶ For they have shed the blood of saints and prophets, And You have given them blood to drink. For it is their just due." ⁷ And I heard another from the altar saying, "Even so, Lord God Almighty, true and righteous *are* Your judgments."

Verses 5–7 provide a pause after the first two judgments are completed. In this pause the murdered tribulation saints along with the angels in heaven are saying these judgments are just and needed upon the evil power and those who follow it.

⁸ Then the fourth angel poured out his bowl on the sun, and power was given to him to scorch men with fire. ⁹ And men were scorched with great heat, and they blasphemed the name of God who has power over these plagues; and they did not repent and give Him glory.

The intensity of the sun's heat was increased. How? Well this is God and He can do it with just a word. Perhaps it was just the movement of the sun closer to the earth or turning the gases up that caused the flames. However, God chooses to turn the temperature up and the sun will become even hotter. The sun's rays will painfully burn the skin of people on earth who have the mark of the beast. Remember those who have the mark of the beast have been inflicted with great sores on their bodies so this intense heat will be extremely painful. In spite of the tremendous pain followers of Satan will not repent. Instead they curse God's name.

¹⁰ Then the fifth angel poured out his bowl on the throne of the beast, and his kingdom became full of darkness; and they gnawed their tongues because of the pain. ¹¹ They blasphemed the God of heaven because of their pains and their sores, and did not repent of their deeds.

Why did they chew their tongues? Think about it. They have very painful sores on their bodies. Their water supply is poisoned. Then the heat from the sun is intensified so that it burns the sores and causes tremendous pain. Then the evil kingdom becomes totally dark. The unsaved are in tremendous pain and life seems hopeless. That's why they chew their tongues but they will not repent.

¹² Then the sixth angel poured out his bowl on the great river Euphrates, and its water was dried up, so that the way of the kings from the east might be prepared.

In the 6th bowl judgment the Kings from the East are allowed to cross over the dried river bed of the Euphrates River in order to have easy access to Israel. The Kings of the East are political leaders from nations east of the Euphrates. Some suggest that the two million man army mentioned in chapter 9 is a Chinese army. But to say this 200 million strong army (Revelation chapter 9) is from the East is to take it out of context. The 200 million strong army are those released from the pit to help Satan carry out evil and fight believers.

Remember the Antichrist violated the peace treaty when he took the city of Jerusalem captive. These kings from the East will come to join the armies of the re-gathered Roman Empire to fight against Israel. As they gather around Israel Christ and His army will appear and they will fight the battle of Armageddon. 1/3 of the world's population has already been killed. Perhaps the 1/3 of the population already dead were people in North America and South America along with other far reaching nations which would explain why they are not specifically mentioned at this battle. We are told that all the armies left on the earth will have assembled here against Israel.

¹³ And I saw three unclean spirits like frogs *coming* out of the mouth of the dragon, out of the mouth of the beast, and out of the mouth of the false prophet.

These unclean spirits are demons. These demons are sent by Satan, the Antichrist and the False Prophet to every leader of the earth and calling them to send their armies to Israel. The armies of the world will respond causing a world war.

¹⁴ For they are spirits of demons, performing signs, *which* go out to the

kings of the earth and of the whole world, to gather them to the battle of that great day of God Almighty.

These demons are given the ability to perform miraculous appearing signs so that these world leaders join the army of the Antichrist against Israel.

¹⁵ "Behold, I am coming as a thief. Blessed *is* he who watches, and keeps his garments, lest he walk naked and they see his shame."

This is given as a warning that Jesus' second coming to earth could happen at any time so it is time to repent and believe in Jesus for salvation rather than be uncovered in the shame of your sins.

¹⁶ And they gathered them together to the place called in Hebrew, Armageddon.

All of the armies make their way to the area around Israel. Armageddon is a Hebrew word without a Greek translation. It is only speculation as to the exact spot where this place will be. The first syllable of Armageddon comes from the Hebrew word meaning mountain. It could be on this mountain the armies will gather and look down of the city ready to attack. In the Hebrew Bible, Megiddo was the name of a fortified city and a plain in northern Palestine. The plain of Megiddo was a kind of natural battlefield and the scene of one notably battle the defeat of King Josiah at the hands of Pharaoh Neco of Egypt (2 Kings 23:29 – 30; 2 Chronicles 35:20 – 24).

¹⁷ Then the seventh angel poured out his bowl into the air, and a loud voice came out of the temple of heaven, from the throne, saying, "It is done!"

It is done! All of the armies have gathered and the stage is set for the Lord's coming to take possession of His Father's earth.

¹⁸ And there were noises and thundering's and lightning's; and there was a great earthquake, such a mighty and great earthquake as had not occurred since men were on the earth.

When the stage was set the worst earthquake that ever happened in history happens accompanied with the sounds of thunder and the sight of lightning occur.

¹⁹ Now the great city was divided into three parts, and the cities of the nations fell. And great Babylon was remembered before God, to give her the cup of the wine of the fierceness of His wrath.

As the armies have gathered around Israel the city of Jerusalem is divided into three sections and the world's political system falls apart. This political system is called Babylon and the evil it has done is remembered by God and she is judged according to her deeds.

[20] Then every island fled away, and the mountains were not found. [21] And great hail from heaven fell upon men, *each hailstone* about the weight of a talent. Men blasphemed God because of the plague of the hail, since that plague was exceedingly great.

The islands have disappeared as well as the mountains. This means that the waters that separated continents have receded and mountains have been leveled. Earth is now one contiguous mass of land centered around Jerusalem (Revelation 21:1 describes this contiguous land). This sets the stage for the millennial kingdom. In the process huge hailstones fall from heaven similar to the plague of Egypt found in Exodus 9:13–35. The hailstones shown to John weighed about 70 pounds each. Under this tremendous judgment they still would not repent. This shows us that God's judgment is just and everyone was given a chance to repent. Each person chose eternal judgement.

SUMMARY: Judgments from the seals on the document in God's hand were executed yet the world still followed the system of whose mark they wore. Then the trumpet judgements sounded which were more intense than the seals and people refused to repent. Here the final set of judgements are being executed and people still won't repent. Not only will they not repent they curse the name of God. There is a parallel between the Exodus of the Hebrews from Egypt and these judgements. God didn't forget His chosen people even though they were captives who had suffered and died at the hands of the Egyptians. God warned the Egyptians through the plagues yet they wouldn't repent. So God caused the Egyptian army to drown in the Red Sea while the Hebrews walked across the dry ground in the parted sea to safety. God's chosen will ultimately cross the parted sea to safety with Jesus while the chosen of Satan die in the flood of Divine judgement.

CHAPTER 16

Revelation Chapter 17

TIMELINE: Time is at the very end of the tribulation. The first three bowls have been poured out. The last four judgments deal with the Antichrist, False Prophet, and Satan, along with all who follow this evil political system. The demons have called all the armies of the world to a place outside of Israel ready for the battle.

Revelation 17:1–18 (NKJV) [1] Then one of the seven angels who had the seven bowls came and talked with me, saying to me, "Come, I will show you the judgment of the great harlot who sits on many waters,

One of the angels who is pouring out the bowl judgements told John to follow him and see the judgments that are about to happen to the world and its political system.

[2] with whom the kings of the earth committed fornication, and the inhabitants of the earth were made drunk with the wine of her fornication."

All of the earth is a part of this world system of the Antichrist. Remember the Antichrist controls the rationing of all commerce around the world which serves as a good incentive to join him.

[3] So he carried me away in the Spirit into the wilderness. And I saw a woman sitting on a scarlet beast *which* was full of names of blasphemy, having seven heads and ten horns. [4] The woman was arrayed in purple and scarlet, and adorned with gold and precious stones and pearls, having in her hand a golden cup full of abominations and the filthiness of her fornication. [5] And on her forehead a name was written: MYSTERY, BABYLON THE GREAT, THE MOTHER OF HARLOTS AND OF THE ABOMINATIONS OF THE EARTH.

John is carried out into the wilderness where he sees a picture of a woman sitting on a red beast. On the beast were the names listing the ways he had blasphemed God. This identifies him as the Antichrist. The beast's seven heads and ten horns identifies the coalition of nations of the revived Roman Empire. On the forehead of the woman was written MYSTERY, BABYLON THE GREAT, THE MOTHER OF HARLOTS AND OF THE ABOMINATIONS OF THE EARTH which identifies her as the political system of the Antichrist. The woman being dressed in purple and scarlet and dressed in a lot of gold and valuable jewels shows the opulence and prosperity of the political system. She has a cup filled showing her open defiance of the word of God and a lifestyle of open and perverted sex.

⁶ I saw the woman, drunk with the blood of the saints and with the blood of the martyrs of Jesus. And when I saw her, I marveled with great amazement. ⁷ But the angel said to me, "Why did you marvel? I will tell you the mystery of the woman and of the beast that carries her, which has the seven heads and the ten horns. ⁸ The beast that you saw was, and is not, and will ascend out of the bottomless pit and go to perdition. And those who dwell on the earth will marvel, whose names are not written in the Book of Life from the foundation of the world, when they see the beast that was, and is not, and yet is.

The Old Roman Empire was in existence during John's time but was not as strong as it had been in previous years. Later the empire imploded from within. The Antichrist will revive it as the center of his world government. But the day is coming when this system will be defeated by Jesus Christ Himself. Those who do not believe in Jesus will marvel at this political system and praise its leader the Antichrist because of its power and wealth.

⁹ Here *is* the mind which has wisdom: The seven heads are seven mountains on which the woman sits.

Here is the truth of what's going on: the capital of the reestablished Roman Empire, and the Antichrist's government, is on the seven mountains that many believe refer to the city of Rome.

¹⁰ There are also seven kings. Five have fallen, one is, *and* the other has not yet come. And when he comes, he must continue a short time.

These seven kings are believed to represent seven great kingdoms that ruled during the history of the earth. Five of them have fallen in defeat at the hand of an outside aggressors. The Ancient Roman Empire is in the process at the time of John's writing of falling apart. It does implode from within and it ceases to be. But when the Antichrist comes into power this old empire will be revived but only for a short time.

¹¹ And the beast that was, and is not, is himself also the eighth, and is of the seven, and is going to perdition.

The leaders in these seven kingdoms were powerful but the 8th, the Antichrist, will be the strongest leader of them all yet he will be defeated.

¹² The ten horns which you saw are ten kings who have received no kingdom as yet, but they receive authority for one hour as kings with the beast.

The ten political leaders or nations have not come into power as John is writing what he sees, but the time is coming when for a short time this political system of the Antichrist will find power over all the nations of earth.

¹³ These are of one mind, and they will give their power and authority to the beast. ¹⁴ These will make war with the Lamb, and the Lamb will overcome them, for He is Lord of lords and King of kings; and those *who are* with Him *are* called, chosen, and faithful."

Remember in chapter 16 that the armies of the world have gathered just outside of Israel. They have been met by their enemy who is causing torment and pain to the people following the Antichrist. This enemy is Jesus Christ and He overcomes them all.

¹⁵ Then he said to me, "The waters which you saw, where the harlot sits, are peoples, multitudes, nations, and tongues.

People from all over the world have gathered and appear as a sea of people. The harlot is the Antichrist's political system in Jerusalem.

¹⁶ And the ten horns which you saw on the beast, these will hate the harlot, make her desolate and naked, eat her flesh and burn her with fire.

¹⁷ For God has put it into their hearts to fulfill His purpose, to be of one mind, and to give their kingdom to the beast, until the words of God are fulfilled.

¹⁸ And the woman whom you saw is that great city which reigns over the kings of the earth."

The nations of the world will turn against the Antichrist at the very end of the tribulation just before Armageddon is fought. They will take his spoils and riches and leave the Antichrist stripped of power. The woman described is this world's political system.

SUMMARY: One of the angels introduces these last four judgements and identifies that they are aimed at the Antichrist and his evil political system.

CHAPTER 17

Revelation Chapter 18

TIMELINE: This chapter takes place at the end of the tribulation period. It is as if John is transported ahead in time and looking back after the political system of the Antichrist and the world's armies are defeated.

Revelation 18:1–24 (NKJV) ¹ After these things I saw another angel coming down from heaven, having great authority, and the earth was illuminated with his glory.

John sees another angel coming down from heaven. This angel had been given great authority to represent God. God's authority in this angel shone like the sun. While this is similar to a description of Christ, it appears to be an angel given authority to represent God in the judgment.

² And he cried mightily with a loud voice, saying, "Babylon the great is fallen, is fallen, and has become a dwelling place of demons, a prison for every foul spirit, and a cage for every unclean and hated bird!

Isaiah and Jeremiah predicted the fall of Babylon which partially was fulfilled in 539 BC by Persia but her permanent destruction will not be fulfilled until this future time. Now that the city has fallen, its inhabitants are dead and all that will be left are demons of every description. The focus now shifts back to pre-destruction.

³ For all the nations have drunk of the wine of the wrath of her fornication, the kings of the earth have committed fornication with her, and the merchants of the earth have become rich through the abundance of her luxury."

When the Antichrist came to power there were great shortages of everything. The Antichrist imposed a rationing system where you had to take his mark in order to buy anything. This appears to answer the need of world hunger so world leaders joined in. Then the economy grew tremendously where everyone who was a part of this rationing system prospered. This made everyone love the Antichrist and saw him as the answer. He gained ultimate authority over the earth.

⁴ And I heard another voice from heaven saying, "Come out of her, my people, lest you share in her sins, and lest you receive of her plagues. ⁵ For her sins have reached to heaven, and God has remembered her iniquities. ⁶ Render to her just as she rendered to you, and repay her double according to her works; in the cup which she has mixed, mix double for her. ⁷ In the measure that she glorified herself and lived luxuriously, in the same measure give her torment and sorrow; for she says in her heart, 'I sit *as* queen, and am no widow, and will not see sorrow. ⁸ Therefore her plagues will come in one day — death and mourning and famine. And she will be utterly burned with fire, for strong *is* the Lord God who judges her.

The warning is sounded to those who refused the mark of the Antichrist, (saved) that they need to run outside of town and hide because the remaining plagues are about to be poured out. If they stay they will feel the effects of the plagues. True believers are poor and persecuted in contrast to those who have the mark who are prosperous and eat well. So the angel announces to true believers that justice is coming. The persecution that you have suffered because of your faith will be given double to those who caused it. In a very short time these plagues will begin which will cause pain, mourning and death. The capital of the political system will be utterly destroyed.

⁹ "The kings of the earth who committed fornication and lived luxuriously with her will weep and lament for her, when they see the smoke of her burning, ¹⁰ standing at a distance for fear of her torment, saying, 'Alas, alas, that great city Babylon, that mighty city! For in one hour your judgment has come.' ¹¹ And the merchants of the earth will weep and mourn over her, for no one buys their merchandise anymore: ¹² merchandise of gold and silver, precious stones and pearls, fine linen and purple, silk and scarlet, every kind of citron wood, every kind of object of ivory, every kind of object of most precious wood, bronze, iron, and marble; ¹³ and cinnamon and incense, fragrant oil and frankincense, wine and oil, fine flour and wheat, cattle and

sheep, horses and chariots, and bodies and souls of men.

The world is devastated. Political leaders see their government destroyed leaving them with no political structure and the great financial boom busted. The rationing system and the universal monetary system have been destroyed. The bodies and souls of men in context here refer to slave trading which is a profitable, yet deplorable, business that exists and will until the millennial reign of Christ.

¹⁴ The fruit that your soul longed for has gone from you, and all the things which are rich and splendid have gone from you, and you shall find them no more at all.

To those who were caught up in the world's system and enjoyed all of its pleasures, it is over. All that you found pleasure and security in is gone forever.

¹⁵ The merchants of these things, who became rich by her, will stand at a distance for fear of her torment, weeping and wailing, ¹⁶ and saying, 'Alas, alas, that great city that was clothed in fine linen, purple, and scarlet, and adorned with gold and precious stones and pearls! ¹⁷ For in one hour such great riches came to nothing. Every shipmaster, all who travel by ship, sailors, and as many as trade on the sea, stood at a distance ¹⁸ and cried out when they saw the smoke of her burning, saying, 'What *is* like this great city?¹⁹ They threw dust on their heads and cried out, weeping and wailing, and saying, 'Alas, alas, that great city, in which all who had ships on the sea became rich by her wealth! For in one hour she is made desolate.

With all that is happening it is hard for people to understand what's going on. Everything is prosperous and great and in just one minute it is destroyed leaving great pain and suffering.

²⁰ Rejoice over her, O heaven, and *you* holy apostles and prophets, for God has avenged you on her!" ²¹ Then a mighty angel took up a stone like a great millstone and threw *it* into the sea, saying, "Thus with violence the great city Babylon shall be thrown down, and shall not be found anymore. ²² The sound of harpists, musicians, flutists, and trumpeters shall not be heard in you anymore. No craftsman of any craft shall be found in you anymore, and the sound of a millstone shall not be heard in you anymore. ²³ The light of a lamp shall not shine in you anymore, and the voice of bridegroom and bride

shall not be heard in you anymore. For your merchants were the great men of the earth, for by your sorcery all the nations were deceived. ²⁴ And in her was found the blood of prophets and saints, and of all who were slain on the earth."

This government, their religious system, and economy are totally destroyed. No sound of happiness is heard on earth. The teachings of God are silent because all of the nations have been deceived and follow Satan's system. The leaders of these nations had caused the death of many prophets and other believers.

SUMMARY: John is shown the outcome when the last of the bowl judgments are poured out. The angel declared that justice would be administered upon those who persecuted believers and blasphemed God. These leaders and the evil system will be destroyed. Hallelujah.

CHAPTER 18

Revelation Chapter 19

TIMELINE: John continues looking ahead to the very end of earth as we know it. As the destruction of this evil government is in sight, chapter 18 verse 20 gave us the perfect command.

18:20 Rejoice over her, O heaven, and *you* holy apostles and prophets, for God has avenged you on her!"

That rejoicing mentioned in chapter 18 is introducing chapter 19.

Revelation 19:1-9 (NKJV) [1] After these things I heard a loud voice of a great multitude in heaven, saying, "Alleluia! Salvation and glory and honor and power *belong* to the Lord our God! [2] For true and righteous *are* His judgments, because He has judged the great harlot who corrupted the earth with her fornication; and He has avenged on her the blood of His servants *shed* by her." [3] Again they said, "Alleluia! Her smoke rises up forever and ever!"

This scene brings to mind Handel's Hallelujah Chorus! In response to the sight of the destruction of evil the multitude in heaven are all saying Alleluia, or hallelujah, salvation and glory and honor and power belong to the Lord our God.

[4] And the twenty-four elders and the four living creatures fell down and worshiped God who sat on the throne, saying, "Amen! Alleluia!" [5] Then a voice came from the throne, saying, "Praise our God, all you His servants and those who fear Him, both small and great!" [6] And I heard, as it were, the voice of a great multitude, as the sound of many waters and as the sound of

mighty thunderings, saying, "Alleluia! For the Lord God Omnipotent reigns!

Now John sees the multitude in heaven—the church and the angels saying alleluias (or hallelujahs), amen (or so be it) to the judgment God has brought because of the sin of earth.

⁷ Let us be glad and rejoice and give Him glory, for the marriage of the Lamb has come, and His wife has made herself ready."

The marriage of the Lamb to the New Testament church appears to happen immediately after the rapture but before the 2nd coming of Christ.

⁸ And to her it was granted to be arrayed in fine linen, clean and bright, for the fine linen is the righteous acts of the saints.

The Bride, the New Testament church, is dressed in righteousness. This righteousness is imputed to them by Christ. Imputing is an act of covering an unrighteous person with the righteousness of Jesus Christ. This is done immediately when a person has saving faith in Jesus Christ. With imputed righteousness a person can come before God and have fellowship with Him.

⁹ Then he said to me, "Write: 'Blessed *are* those who are called to the marriage supper of the Lamb!'" And he said to me, "These are the true sayings of God."

The marriage supper or feast is a subject of a lot of speculation. It appears to happen after the rapture and after the marriage ceremony and consummation have been completed. The supper's placement fits during the seven years of tribulation on the earth. Christ and his bride during this time are having special fellowship. While the souls of Old Testament saints and tribulation saints are in heaven in the protection and safety of God, we are not given any word of their having received their glorified bodies yet like the church saints did at the rapture. They are in a state like church saints who died before the rapture were in until they received their heavenly bodies at the rapture.

What is the consummation of Christ and the church? Because all we have to draw from are the traditions of marriage in Christ's time and our understanding of marriage, we only have assumptions about the consummation. The New Testament church will receive rewards for acts of obedience to Christ just after they are raptured. It appears that the church will present their rewards to Christ as an act of our love which could be the consummation of the marriage. Revelation 4:9 show leaders of the church bowing down to worship and presenting their crowns to Christ because He is worthy. Many assume this to be the church giving her rewards to Christ as an act of love.

The Bride and Groom will be the purpose of the feast so who is being called to attend the feast? Daniel tells us about some who will be called.

Daniel 12:1–2 (NKJV) [1] "At that time Michael (an archangel) shall stand up, The great prince who stands *watch* over the sons of your people; (Michael stands guard over Israel) And there shall be a time of trouble, [this is prophecy of the seven years of the tribulation] Such as never was since there was a nation, (worst pain and trouble ever seen) *Even* to that time. And at that time your people shall be delivered, Every one who is found written in the book. [Jews and everyone who were saved in Old Testament days] [2] And many of those who sleep in the dust of the earth shall awake, (all the dead except the saved who had died during church age who, according to 1 Thessalonians 4, are raised at the rapture) Some to everlasting life, Some to shame *and* everlasting contempt.

The Bible tells us that the saved during the church age will be changed in the rapture and given their eternal bodies. They are worshiping Christ and fellowshipping with Him in heaven. John sees the martyred saints from the Tribulation under the altar not having been given eternal bodies yet but in the complete safety and protection of God. Old Testament saints when they die are in heaven and there is no record of their having received their eternal bodies yet. These saints from the Old Testament day and Tribulation who have not received their eternal bodies yet seem to be the ones called to the marriage supper. They are awaiting their eternal bodies until after the millennial kingdom as they are ushered into eternity. What they are clothed in before they receive their heavenly body? We are not told. Perhaps a temporary body. Some believe the soul is at sleep until receiving their heavenly body but we see tribulation saints under the altar awake and not sleeping. They base this on the references to saints who have died as at rest or asleep. One day we will know for sure.

Revelation 19:10 ¹⁰ And I fell at his feet to worship him. But he said to me, "See *that you do not do that!* I am your fellow servant, and of your brethren who have the testimony of Jesus. Worship God! For the testimony of Jesus is the spirit of prophecy."

John is so overtaken with joy that he falls down at the feet of the angel and begins to worship. The angel has to remind John that worship is reserved for Jesus because He is the One responsible for what John is seeing.

¹¹ Now I saw heaven opened, and behold, a white horse. And He who sat on him *was* called Faithful and True, and in righteousness He judges and makes war. ¹² His eyes *were* like a flame of fire, and on His head *were* many crowns. He had a name written that no one knew except Himself. ¹³ He *was* clothed with a robe dipped in blood, and His name is called The Word of God. ¹⁴ And the armies in heaven, clothed in fine linen, white and clean, followed Him on white horses.

John sees Jesus on a white horse preparing for war against Satan, the Antichrist, and the evil world system. Behind Him is His army who is Christ's righteous bride on white horses. They leave heaven to take possession of earth.

¹⁵ Now out of His mouth goes a sharp sword, that with it He should strike the nations. And He Himself will rule them with a rod of iron. He Himself treads the winepress of the fierceness and wrath of Almighty God. ¹⁶ And He has on *His* robe and on His thigh a name written: KING OF KINGS AND LORD OF LORDS.

Jesus and His army reach earth and He opens His mouth and a sword goes out. What is the sword in Jesus' mouth? It is the Word of God. Hebrew 4:12 tells us that God's Word is sharper than a two-edged sword and Ephesians 6:17 tells us that the sword of the spirit is the Word of God. Jesus will speak the Word of God, which will judge the world of her sin.

Being just, Jesus will deliver divine, sure justice because of the world's unforgiven sin. His judgment will be fierce and complete because of the nature of their sin. On Jesus' robe is written King of Kings and Lord of Lords, which shows that He has the authority to bring this judgment on sin. Jesus is taking His place as the ultimate King, ready to rule from the throne of David forever as had been promised.

¹⁷ Then I saw an angel standing in the sun; and he cried with a loud voice, saying to all the birds that fly in the midst of heaven, "Come and gather together for the supper of the great God, ¹⁸ that you may eat the flesh of kings, the flesh of captains, the flesh of mighty men, the flesh of horses and of those who sit on them, and the flesh of all *people*, free and slave, both small and great."

The angel standing in the sun announces the death of all kings and people of earth by calling all of the birds of the air to come and feast on the dead kings and all people of earth.

¹⁹ And I saw the beast, the kings of the earth, and their armies, gathered together to make war against Him who sat on the horse and against His army.

This final battle of the war, the battle of Armageddon, is taking place.

²⁰ Then the beast was captured, and with him the false prophet who worked signs in his presence, by which he deceived those who received the mark of the beast and those who worshiped his image. These two were cast alive into the lake of fire burning with brimstone. ²¹ And the rest were killed with the sword which proceeded from the mouth of Him who sat on the horse. And all the birds were filled with their flesh.

This battle will only last a minute. Jesus speaks and every king and every soldier of the earth and all who followed them are killed. Jesus captures Satan, the Antichrist, and the false prophet. The Antichrist and the false prophet are the first to be cast into the lake of fire. Satan will be bound and thrown into the bottomless pit.

SUMMARY: John has seen the marriage of Jesus to His church. The saved of the Old Testament age are invited to the marriage feast which will last for seven years. Then he sees Jesus and His army, which is His bride, leave heaven on white horses. They engage battle with everyone on earth. Jesus speaks and all of the armies of the world and their political leaders are dead. The Antichrist and false prophet are sent to the lake of fire, Satan is bound and locked up for 1,000 years and the Tribulation saints are sent to Jesus as the New City of Jerusalem comes to earth. The dead on earth are sent to the place of death waiting for the Great White Throne Judgement.

CHAPTER 19

Revelation Chapter 20

TIMELINE: Time is just after the Antichrist and the False Prophet have been sent to the lake of fire and all of the evil armies of the world have been killed. Then time moves forward to the end of the one thousand year kingdom.

Revelation 20:1–15 (NKJV) [1] Then I saw an angel coming down from heaven, having the key to the bottomless pit and a great chain in his hand.

The bottomless pit is not the same as the lake of fire. It is in hell but it is in a different part of hell because the lake of fire will be the eternal destination of Satan and everyone who followed him. Just like the angels that left their proper domain were cast into the bottomless pit and released many centuries later during the tribulation to help Satan inflict pain on believers so will Satan be released after 1,000 years. The only ones who have been cast into the lake of fire so far are the Antichrist and the False Prophet.

[2] He laid hold of the dragon, that serpent of old, who is *the* Devil and Satan, and bound him for a thousand years; [3] and he cast him into the bottomless pit, and shut him up, and set a seal on him, so that he should deceive the nations no more till the thousand years were finished. But after these things he must be released for a little while.

During the thousand years of the Millennial, Jesus and His bride are ruling the earth from the New City of Jerusalem. Jesus fulfills the prophecy concerning His ruling from the throne of David over the Jews in a time of unprecedented peace. Peace because there is no evidence of sin since the curse of sin has been cleansed, and Satan and his demons are locked up.

But after this 1,000 years is over the chains are removed and Satan will be released to roam earth for a short time.

⁴ And I saw thrones, and they sat on them, and judgment was committed to them. Then *I saw* the souls of those who had been beheaded for their witness to Jesus and for the word of God, who had not worshiped the beast or his image, and had not received *his* mark on their foreheads or on their hands. And they lived and reigned with Christ for a thousand years. ⁵ But the rest of the dead did not live again until the thousand years were finished. This *is* the first resurrection.

The kings of the revived Roman Empire political coalition have been judged for their wickedness and for killing believers. Those tribulation saints, people who were saved during the tribulation, will come into the Millennial Kingdom for the entire 1,000 years. Everyone else who died during the tribulation will stay in the place of death until the millennial is over.

⁶ Blessed and holy *is* he who has part in the first resurrection. Over such the second death has no power, but they shall be priests of God and of Christ, and shall reign with Him a thousand years.

The first resurrection refers to the church at the rapture and carried to Christ. It also refers to Old Testament saints and tribulation saints who immediately are carried to God at death and will remain in His care until eternity. While during the tribulation God is primarily working with Jews, many Gentiles will be saved as well. These tribulation believers are carried into the Millennial Kingdom after Armageddon to fulfill the prophecy that the Messiah will rule over Israel from the throne of David in absolute peace. Here the first resurrection is the dead from the church who, at the rapture, have been changed into heavenly bodies and Old Testament saints and martyred tribulation saints who are in the care of God. All of the saved before the final battle between Satan and Christ make up the first resurrection. The second resurrection will be the unsaved from all ages brought to stand before God at the Great White Throne Judgment.

⁷ Now when the thousand years have expired, Satan will be released from his prison ⁸ and will go out to deceive the nations which are in the four corners of the earth, Gog and Magog, to gather them together to battle, whose number *is* as the sand of the sea.

When Satan is released from the bottomless pit after the 1,000 years is over he will move all over the earth with his demons tempting people to sin. Those who choose to follow Satan will be gathered with Satan back to the place where the battle of Gog and Magog was fought. There Satan will seek a rematch — another battle with Christ. Satan's army is going to be huge.

Who are these people who have joined forces with Satan? That is left to speculation. Some believe children will be born to the tribulation saints during the thousand years of the Millennium. Because they were born with no influence of sin at all around them, they have never been tempted to sin. When Satan appears they will be tempted to follow him instead of King Jesus. They have to choose obedience to Christ or fall to the temptation of Satan and join his army.

Others believe that Satan will go into the place of death and gather his army. Or perhaps those who died unsaved during the tribulation were cast into the bottomless pit with Satan and are released with him. Still others believe that the demon army Satan used to inflict pain during the tribulation will again join Satan to form this army.

The Bible does not gives us details about who makes up this army because that is not the focus. The focus is that Satan will make one last attempt to defeat God but is eternally defeated and cast into the lake of fire. Hallelujah!

⁹ They went up on the breadth of the earth and surrounded the camp of the saints and the beloved city. And fire came down from God out of heaven and devoured them.

This is where Satan gathers his army to challenge Christ again. When he does fire falls from heaven and destroys Satan and his army.

¹⁰ The devil, who deceived them, was cast into the lake of fire and brimstone where the beast and the false prophet *are*. And they will be tormented day and night forever and ever.

Immediately after his defeat, Satan is cast in the lake of fire where the Antichrist and the False Prophet were thrown after the tribulation. They are the only three there right now. John sees the lake of fire as a place where there is torment for eternity.

¹¹ Then I saw a great white throne and Him who sat on it, from whose face

the earth and the heaven fled away. And there was found no place for them. ¹² And I saw the dead, small and great, standing before God, and books were opened. And another book was opened, which is *the Book* of Life. And the dead were judged according to their works, by the things which were written in the books. ¹³ The sea gave up the dead who were in it, and Death and Hades delivered up the dead who were in them. And they were judged, each one according to his works. ¹⁴ Then Death and Hades were cast into the lake of fire. This is the second death. ¹⁵ And anyone not found written in the Book of Life was cast into the lake of fire.

After Satan is cast into the lake of fire a great white throne appears. God is sitting on this throne and unsaved people from every age will stand before God. God has before Him books. What are these books? It appears that these books are the law of God. God's standard of righteousness. Then another book is opened which is identified as the Book of Life. The book of life is the registry of all of those who belong to Jesus Christ. The saved of every age.

Why these books? Because the only way to go to heaven is to be absolutely righteous. The law is God's standard of righteousness. Everyone would be judged by whether they were righteous or not. If they had ever violated God's law — sinned — they are not righteous. So none of them will be righteous. The only other way to righteousness is to have Christ impute or totally cover you with His righteousness. Yet everyone standing before God at this judgment have never accepted Jesus imputed righteousness. So no one was found righteous. No one could enter heaven. The Bible tells us then they were cast into the lake of fire. It says these unsaved people were cast into Hell which is called Death and Hades because the Bible declares a person is dead in their sins if they have not received Jesus' imputed righteousness. Hades means the place of the dead — where the dead are. "This is the second death," means that they will be separated from God for eternity. Just like salvation is the second birth, damnation is the second death.

SUMMARY: After the 1,000 year Millennial Kingdom is over, Satan is released from the bottomless pit. He immediately starts to go all over the world to gather an army. Remember Christ and His bride are living in the New City of Jerusalem where Jesus is ruling from the throne of David. The surface of the world was changed after the battle of Armageddon, and now all the land of the world is contiguous—it is not separated by water into continents.. After Satan is released from the bottomless pit he gathers his army very quickly and he leads them to Megiddo where he was defeated 1,000 years before, for a rematch. Satan is immediately defeated again and is cast into the lake of fire. Then a white throne appears and God, the great judge, seats on that throne. Everyone one who has ever lived (Old Testament and New Testament times) and has not accepted Jesus Christ stands before God to be judged. God has books in front of Him and everyone who is not found in the Lamb's book of life is judged and cast into the lake of fire.

CHAPTER 20

Revelation Chapter 21

TIMELINE: Time moves back to just after the tribulation and just before the Millennial Kingdom. Satan has been locked up in the bottomless pit for 1,000 years. John sees the New City of Jerusalem coming into place on the earth where Jerusalem is located today.

Revelation 21:1–27 (NKJV) [1] Now I saw a new heaven and a new earth, for the first heaven and the first earth had passed away. Also there was no more sea.

Earth's surface and the sky above the earth had to be purified from the curse of sin before this holy city could be moved into its place. All of the seas are gone and earth is just one contiguous stretch of land with the city of Jerusalem at the very center.

[2] Then I, John, saw the holy city, New Jerusalem, coming down out of heaven from God, prepared as a bride adorned for her husband. [3] And I heard a loud voice from heaven saying, "Behold, the tabernacle of God *is* with men, and He will dwell with them, and they shall be His people. God Himself will be with them *and be* their God.

After the land had been cleansed this city prepared in heaven came down to earth. It appears to sit just where the city of Jerusalem sits today because this is where the throne of David will sit to rule Israel. It is much bigger than today's city. In the city there is a new temple which is not a building but Christ Himself. Remember the tabernacle and later the temple housed the ark of the covenant which represented the presence of God with His people. Christ will represent God's presence in the city.

⁴ And God will wipe away every tear from their eyes; there shall be no more death, nor sorrow, nor crying. There shall be no more pain, for the former things have passed away." ⁵ Then He who sat on the throne said, "Behold, I make all things new." And He said to me, "Write, for these words are true and faithful."

Everything is different now because the curse of sin is gone. No more pain, death, sorrow or crying. Jesus Christ said that He made everything perfect and the imperfect is destroyed. This, Christ said, is a promise that you can depend on.

⁶ And He said to me, "It is done! I am the Alpha and the Omega, the Beginning and the End. I will give of the fountain of the water of life freely to him who thirsts. ⁷ He who overcomes shall inherit all things, and I will be his God and he shall be My son.

God said, I have completed My promise. The triune God was in the beginning before anything was created. I am the source of life itself, He says. Everyone who accepts Jesus Christ's offer of salvation by true believing faith will inherit everything I have and will become My child.

⁸ But the cowardly, unbelieving, abominable, murderers, sexually immoral, sorcerers, idolaters, and all liars shall have their part in the lake which burns with fire and brimstone, which is the second death."

Everyone with unforgiven sin will be cast into the lake of fire with Satan and will face continual torment and the permanent separation from God.

⁹ Then one of the seven angels who had the seven bowls filled with the seven last plagues came to me and talked with me, saying, "Come, I will show you the bride, the Lamb's wife."

One of these seven angels who will unleash these seven last plagues told John to go with him to see this New City of Jerusalem. John describes what this beautiful city will look like.

¹⁰ And he carried me away in the Spirit to a great and high mountain, and showed me the great city, the holy Jerusalem, descending out of heaven from God, ¹¹ having the glory of God. Her light *was* like a most precious stone, like a jasper stone, clear as crystal.

The glory of God appears as a pure light that glimmered like light shining through a very fine diamond.

¹² Also she had a great and high wall with twelve gates, and twelve angels at the gates, and names written on them, which are *the names* of the twelve tribes of the children of Israel: ¹³ three gates on the east, three gates on the north, three gates on the south, and three gates on the west.

This city has huge walls around it. These walls around the city had twelve gates with the names of the twelve tribes of Israel written on them. Three gates on the south, Three gates on the North, Three gates on the West, and Three gates on the East. The names of the tribes of Israel represent that Israel will have access to Jesus who will rule over Israel during this time. Everyone will have access to the throne of David but God promised that Jesus would reign over Israel forever (2 Samuel 7:12–16).

¹⁴ Now the wall of the city had twelve foundations, and on them were the names of the twelve apostles of the Lamb.

The foundation of the wall had twelve sections or layers and on each layer there was a name of one of the twelve apostles of Christ. This seems to show that this city was built for the New Testament church, the bride, but Israel will have complete access to her King who sits on the throne of authority over Israel.

¹⁵ And he who talked with me had a gold reed to measure the city, its gates, and its wall. ¹⁶ The city is laid out as a square; its length is as great as its breadth. And he measured the city with the reed: twelve thousand furlongs. Its length, breadth, and height are equal. ¹⁷ Then he measured its wall: one hundred *and* forty-four cubits, *according* to the measure of a man, that is, of an angel.

John is shown the magnitude of this great city. It is about 1400 miles from east to west and about 1400 miles from north to south. It also extends about 1400 miles into the sky.

¹⁸ The construction of its wall was *of* jasper; and the city *was* pure gold, like clear glass. ¹⁹ The foundations of the wall of the city were adorned with all kinds of precious stones: the first foundation *was* jasper, the second sapphire, the third chalcedony, the fourth emerald, ²⁰ the fifth sardonyx, the sixth sardius, the seventh chrysolite, the eighth beryl, the ninth topaz, the tenth chrysoprase, the eleventh jacinth, and the twelfth amethyst. ²¹ The twelve gates *were* twelve pearls: each individual gate was of one pearl. And the street of the city *was* pure gold, like transparent glass.

The walls were pure translucent gold and the light of the glory of Christ glistened through them. The foundation was studded with millions of precious jewels. Each of the twelve gates were made from one huge flawless Pearl. The street is made of pure gold like the walls. It is supposed that this one street comes from each of the twelve gates and leads to the throne of David where Jesus sits.

²² But I saw no temple in it, for the Lord God Almighty and the Lamb are its temple. ²³ The city had no need of the sun or of the moon to shine in it, for the glory of God illuminated it. The Lamb *is* its light.

The glory of God through Jesus is always seen by humans as a bright pure light. There won't be a need to have the sun or moon to give us light because the radiance of God's glory reflected through His Son will be sufficient that everyone can see. They will be guided by His light.

²⁴ And the nations of those who are saved shall walk in its light, and the kings of the earth bring their glory and honor into it.

The term nations are all of the saved except the New Testament church. There will evidently be organization and political leaders in these nations outside of the city. Because sin is gone these leaders will lead perfectly with no self-righteousness or self-pride. They will rule under Jesus Christ's and His bride's authority in a way that will bring glory and honor to Him.

²⁵ Its gates shall not be shut at all by day (there shall be no night there). ²⁶ And they shall bring the glory and the honor of the nations into it.

Every nation will have access to King Jesus at all times. They love the King and will seek to bring him glory and honor through all that is done in the nations.

²⁷ But there shall by no means enter it anything that defiles, or causes an abomination or a lie, but only those who are written in the Lamb's Book of Life.

SUMMARY: John is carried back before chapter 20 to see details about the city that has been prepared for the bride of Christ. John sees the city that has descended to the earth from God's heaven. He describes the beautiful jewels of the foundation, the gates made of a single pure pearl. He sees the walls and a street made of a translucent pure gold. This city was 1400 miles long, wide and high. The gates were open giving access into the city and the King to the perfect world. John sees the source of light for the earth as the glory of God through Jesus.

John is told that during the Millennial Kingdom, because Satan is locked up in the bottomless pit and the curse of sin has been removed, there is no influence of evil found anywhere. What does it mean that the curse of sin is gone? Sin brought a curse when Adam had sinned. God said that because of sin the serpent, which housed the presence of Satan, could no longer stand-up but would have to crawl on his belly. He would be feared and hated by people. In this kingdom there will be no need to fear any snake and possibly they will be able to stand again.

The curse given to the woman was that she would be in great pain during her pregnancy and then in giving birth to her children. It went on to say that she would have a need to be emotionally attached to someone, her husband, and she would have a deep need to follow the leadership of her husband even though she would want to rebel against it.

To the man he would have to labor hard to make a living. While that struggle in making a living changes through the ages, there is a struggle in making a living. During the Millennial Kingdom it will be like it was during the Garden of Eden before Adam sinned. Adam and Eve were given jobs to dress the garden. Everyone will work in the Millennial Kingdom but will do so without stress and difficulties. Because Satan is locked up no one will be tempted in any way to rebel, or hurt or to be selfish. The Millennial Kingdom will be a perfect environment.

CHAPTER 21

Revelation Chapter 22

TIMELINE: John is still being shown details of the city. The timeline then shifts from the Millennial Kingdom to Eternity. After the Millennial Kingdom Satan will be released and he will contaminate the earth with a battle against Christ. The New City of Jerusalem and every one of the inhabitants of the kingdom will ascend into God's heaven.

Revelation 22:1–17 (NKJV) [1] And he showed me a pure river of water of life, clear as crystal, proceeding from the throne of God and of the Lamb.

Here John sees the river of the water of life and it is absolutely pure and as clear as crystal. It descends from the thrones of God and His Son Jesus Christ. What is the river of the water of life? It appears to represent the source of eternal life given to all who come to heaven. Just like water is absolutely needed to sustain life, Jesus is absolutely needed for spiritual life.

[2] In the middle of its street, and on either side of the river, *was* the tree of life, which bore twelve fruits, each *tree* yielding its fruit every month. The leaves of the tree *were* for the healing of the nations.

Here is the picture that John is seeing. He sees in the background the thrones of God and Jesus. From these thrones, John sees this river flowing through the middle of the city. On both sides of the river John sees the trees of life. It appears that there are twelve trees of the tree of life which continually bears fruit. There were twelve apostles in the New Testament and twelve tribes of Israel in the Old Testament. This shows heaven is for every saved person from every time of history and every nationality.

[3] And there shall be no more curse, but the throne of God and of the Lamb shall be in it, and His servants shall serve Him.

As mentioned in the last chapter the curse of sin is gone. Now serving God the Father and His Son Jesus Christ's will be the dominant desire in everybody.

⁴ They shall see His face, and His name *shall be* on their foreheads.

Everyone will be able to see God and He will have His name on their heads. This is a contrast to the name of the Antichrist on everyone who followed him during the tribulation which lasted only a short time. The name of God will last for eternity.

⁵ There shall be no night there: They need no lamp nor light of the sun, for the Lord God gives them light. And they shall reign forever and ever. ⁶ Then he said to me, "These words *are* faithful and true." And the Lord God of the holy prophets sent His angel to show His servants the things which must shortly take place. ⁷ "Behold, I am coming quickly! Blessed *is* he who keeps the words of the prophecy of this book."

As in the new city on earth is lighted by the glory of God so it will be in heaven. In heaven, everyone will rule and reign with God and Jesus forever and ever. He says God promised that this will happen. And even though the years may seem like a long time in human comprehension, but in God's time it is only a short time before it will take place.

⁸ Now I, John, saw and heard these things. And when I heard and saw, I fell down to worship before the feet of the angel who showed me these things.

John says that he was an eyewitness. He actually saw everything that he wrote in this book. As John realized what the angel was showing him the thought of it made him fall down and worship.

⁹ Then he said to me, "See *that you do* not *do that*. For I am your fellow servant, and of your brethren the prophets, and of those who keep the words of this book. Worship God."

The angel said stop that. Don't worship me, worship God. I am just doing what God wanted me to do.

¹⁰ And he said to me, "Do not seal the words of the prophecy of this book, for the time is at hand.

The angel was saying, "John, don't keep what you have seen to yourself. You need to write it down and give it to people to warn them that the time for these things have come."

¹¹ He who is unjust, let him be unjust still; he who is filthy, let him be filthy

still; he who is righteous, let him be righteous still; he who is holy, let him be holy still."

Eternity is too late to make a difference.

¹² "And behold, I am coming quickly, and My reward *is* with Me, to give to every one according to his work. ¹³ I am the Alpha and the Omega, *the* Beginning and *the* End, the First and the Last." ¹⁴ Blessed *are* those who do His commandments, that they may have the right to the tree of life, and may enter through the gates into the city. ¹⁵ But outside *are* dogs and sorcerers and sexually immoral and murderers and idolaters, and whoever loves and practices a lie.

The reward for our work will be just after the rapture. Salvation is not a reward for our works, it is a gift from God. **Ephesians 2:8 (NKJV) tells us:** ⁸ For by grace you have been saved through faith, and that not of yourselves; *it is* the gift of God.

Doing His commandments talks about obedience to His instruction to believe on the Lord Jesus Christ for salvation. Only people who are obedient to the call of the Holy Spirit to be saved will have access to the tree of life.

¹⁶ "I, Jesus, have sent My angel to testify to you these things in the churches. I am the Root and the Offspring of David, the Bright and Morning Star." ¹⁷ And the Spirit and the bride say, "Come!" And let him who hears say, "Come!" And let him who thirsts come. Whoever desires, let him take the water of life freely.

Jesus testifies He was the one who sent the angel as His representative and that everything here is true. Jesus, through the Holy Spirit, sends an invitation to everyone to accept His salvation. When a person does accept Christ's invitation he will have complete access to the water and trees of life eternally.

SUMMARY: In this chapter John is given a look into eternity. He sees the new city of Jerusalem but this time it is in heaven again. He sees the throne of Jesus as he did when the city was on earth but in addition he now sees the throne of God as well. John is assured that a person's destiny in eternity is set forever — it can't be changed. Those who have trusted Christ and received His righteousness will be in God's presence for eternity. However, those who are not found in the Lamb's book of Life which contain the names of those forgiven and covered with Christ's righteous, will be in the lake of fire forever.

CHAPTER 22

Timing of the End Time Events

When will all of these judgments and tribulations begin? In Matthew 24 Jesus was walking with His disciples and they were showing Him the beauty of the temple. Jesus responded to them with a short-term prophecy.

Matthew 24:2 (NKJV) 2 And Jesus said to them, "Do you not see all these things? Assuredly, I say to you, not one stone shall be left here upon another, that shall not be thrown down."

Jesus was talking about the temple. History tells us that in 70 AD Nero, the Roman emperor, sent Titus, a Roman general, to Jerusalem to stop what he thought was a rebellion by the Jews. Titus, known as a mad man, led 80,000 Roman soldiers into the city. His anger was so intense that his army destroyed everything. In destroying the temple he not only knocked it down, he made sure not one stone was left on top of another. Titus thought he was showing these Jews who was in charge, but in reality he was just fulfilling this prophecy spoken by Jesus some 40 years earlier.

This short-term prophecy was completely fulfilled just as it was given which is a guarantee, a first fruit, that all prophecy will be fulfilled exactly as it has been given. Then the disciples asked for signs that the end and Jesus second coming was beginning. Jesus gave signs that will precede His coming. He said that these signs will be like birth pains in that they will hit and go away and over a period of time they will begin to hit harder and harder and happen faster and faster until they usher in the birth of judgment.

These are the signs that Jesus gave the Disciples that the end times had begun:

Matthew 24:4–51 (NKJV) ⁴ And Jesus answered and said to them: "Take heed that no one deceives you. ⁵ For many will come in My name, saying, 'I am the Christ,' and will deceive many.

Many people through the years have come as prophets and preachers of Jesus Christ but present a false gospel. Jesus warns about this deception. Ultimately during the tribulation the Antichrist will be accepted as a false Messiah.

⁶ And you will hear of wars and rumors of wars. See that you are not troubled; for all these things must come to pass, but the end is not yet.

There have been times of wars and rumors of wars through the years. This would be more specifically speaking about wars in the Middle East and around Israel which is a hot spot of tension today.

⁷ For nation will rise against nation, and kingdom against kingdom. And there will be famines, pestilences, and earthquakes in various places. ⁸ All these are the beginning of sorrows.

Through the years there have been periods of great wars and times of catastrophic acts of nature in strange places. According to the pattern of birth pains these wars and catastrophic acts will grow in intensity and timing. The war described in Psalm 83 and then the war described in Ezekiel 38, 39 will bring in the birth of the tribulation. Then the Bible describes famines, pestilences, and earthquakes upon the area around Israel.

Jesus then describes what can be expected until his second coming.

⁹ Then they will deliver you up to tribulation and kill you, and you will be hated by all nations for My name's sake. ¹⁰ And then many will be offended, will betray one another, and will hate one another. ¹¹ Then many false prophets will rise up and deceive many. ¹² And because lawlessness will abound, the love of many will grow cold. ¹³ But he who endures to the end shall be saved. ¹⁴ And this gospel of the kingdom will be preached in all the world as a witness to all the nations, and then the end will come.

During the church age, the period between Jesus ascension and the beginning of the tribulation, there will be times of persecution and troubles for the church. These signs will intensify and accelerate in occurrence leading into the first half of the tribulation. Then in verse 15 time moves to the middle of the Tribulation to the abomination of desolation and the woes that follow.

¹⁵ "Therefore when you see the 'abomination of desolation,' spoken of by Daniel the prophet, standing in the holy place" (whoever reads, let him understand), ¹⁶ then let those who are in Judea flee to the mountains. ¹⁷ Let him who is on the housetop not go down to take anything out of his house. ¹⁸ And let him who is in the field not go back to get his clothes. ¹⁹ But woe to those who are pregnant and to those who are nursing babies in those days! ²⁰ And pray that your flight may not be in winter or on the Sabbath. ²¹ For then there will be great tribulation, such as has not been since the beginning of the world until this time, no, nor ever shall be. ²² And unless those days were shortened, no flesh would be saved; but for the elect's sake those days will be shortened.

During the last half of the tribulation the woes will increase and be so intense that believers are warned to flee to places outside of Judea where God will take care of and offer them safety. Verses 23 through 32 go on to describe the terrible woes and the difficulty believers will have as non-believers are tormented and the earth is destroyed under the great judgment.

³³ So you also, when you see all these things, know that it is near — at the doors! ³⁴ Assuredly, I say to you, this generation will by no means pass away till all these things take place.

The generation alive during the tribulation will endure all of the woes.

³⁵ heaven and earth will pass away, but My words will by no means pass away. ³⁶ "But of that day and hour no one knows, not even the angels of heaven, but My Father only.

All of God's promises and all prophecies about the end will come to being just as they were given. We have signs of the conditions leading to the end, which will come and go throughout the church age and will grow in frequency and intensity until the tribulation begins. We just don't know the exact time this period of judgments will begin. Matthew continues to share some signs leading up to the tribulation by comparing the end to the time that Noah lived.

³⁷ But as the days of Noah were, so also will the coming of the Son of Man be. ³⁸ For as in the days before the flood, they were eating and drinking, marrying and giving in marriage, until the day that Noah entered the ark, ³⁹ and did not know until the flood came and took them all away, so also will the coming of the Son of Man be.

Life will be going on just like normal people partying and living life until the exact time that judgment is ready. Then events of the rapture are explained.

⁴⁰ Then two men will be in the field: one will be taken and the other left. ⁴¹ Two women will be grinding at the mill: one will be taken and the other left. ⁴² Watch therefore, for you do not know what hour your Lord is coming.

Then admonition is given to get ready now and be watching for the rapture.

⁴³ But know this, that if the master of the house had known what hour the thief would come, he would have watched and not allowed his house to be broken into. ⁴⁴ Therefore you also be ready, for the Son of Man is coming at an hour you do not expect. ⁴⁵ "Who then is a faithful and wise servant, whom his master made ruler over his household, to give them food in due season? ⁴⁶ Blessed is that servant whom his master, when he comes, will find so doing. ⁴⁷ Assuredly, I say to you that he will make him ruler over all his goods. ⁴⁸ But if that evil servant says in his heart, 'My master is delaying his coming,' ⁴⁹ and begins to beat his fellow servants, and to eat and drink with the drunkards, ⁵⁰ the master of that servant will come on a day when he is not looking for him and at an hour that he is not aware of, ⁵¹ and will cut him in two and appoint him his portion with the hypocrites. There shall be weeping and gnashing of teeth.

The book of Revelation was given by the authority of God the Father to Jesus His Son who gave it to John to record for mankind. Because of this it carries the weight of God's reputation for truth and accuracy. As Matthew declares it will come to pass as it has been written.

Actually, the signs of the end began just after Jesus left earth and went to heaven. The Apostle Paul apparently believed he was living in the last days because of the signs he saw. Birth pains appear and then they disappear. After a while they reappear and this process happens over and over again until the pains begin to happen very fast, very often and very hard. So, every generation of the church age is going to see some of these signs. Seeing these signs should remind us to live in a state of expectancy of the rapture. So, all through the church age people are living in the last days.

While we don't know the exact placement of the end time events here is a quick list of what is to come before the end. A war described in Psalm 83 will be fought against Israel. Israel wins. This war appears to be won quickly. A war described in Ezekiel chapters 38 and 39 is fought. It appears to begin very quickly after the Psalm 83 war is over. God gives Israel a miraculous victory.

The Antichrist leads in signing a peace treaty for seven years with Israel which brings him into a leadership position over ten nations in a revival of the Old Roman Empire.

The rapture of the church occurs. All true believers from the church age are taken to heaven.

144,000 Jews are saved and dedicate their lives to witnessing to the world about Jesus. They are sealed so that they cannot be killed until their ministry is over.

Condition on the earth are difficult. The Antichrist will enforce a system of commerce that require his mark in order to purchase anything.

After 3 1/2 years the Antichrist will break the seven year peace treaty that he led in signing. He will invade Jerusalem and take charge of the temple where the False Prophet will direct worship of the Antichrist. All sacrifice and worship to God will cease and the Antichrist will blaspheme the name of God. When the temple is desecrated the worst pains and woes that the world has ever experienced will begin. Two witnesses with power to perform certain miracles and shoot fire from their mouths to kill anyone who would harm them will come from God. They will witness of Jesus for 1260 days and then God will allow them to be killed. Their dead bodies will lay in the streets of Jerusalem for 3 1/2 days as the world watches and rejoices. After 3 1/2 days God will breathe life back into the witnesses and then call them into heaven as the world watches. For the next few days after the witnesses die, all of the armies of the nations left on earth will ascend toward Israel for a great battle. That battle will lead to the battle of Armageddon where Jesus will speak and defeat every army, every leader, the Antichrist, the False Prophet, and every unsaved person alive.

The Antichrist and False Prophet are cast into the lake of fire for eternity. Satan will be chained and cast into the bottomless pit for 1,000 years.

The unsaved of the tribulation are sent to the place of death where all unsaved of every generation are being held.

All of the elements of earth and the atmosphere above earth will be cleansed from the effects of the curse of sin. The seas will disappear, and the mountains will be moved to make room for the tribulation saints to live.

Those saved from the Tribulation, will join Jesus Christ and His bride, the church, and go into the new heavens and earth. There they will find the new city of Jerusalem. There will be no sin, no sickness, and no death for 1,000 years.

Then Satan is released from the bottomless pit. He gathers an army and challenges Christ again and is immediately defeated again. Then Satan will be cast into the lake of fire for eternity.

All of the unsaved from every generation will be taken from the place of death and stand before the great White Throne of God to be judged. Because they are not righteous and their names are not in the Lamb's book of Life they will all be cast into the lake of fire for eternity. Remember God will not banish them into hell — their sin and their choice not to accept Jesus' offer of salvation sends them to the lake of fire.

Then all of the saved from every generation will go to live with God at His home in heaven. Praise the Lord!